# The Lost Warship

*by*

Robert Moore Williams

**The Lost Warship**
**by Robert Moore Williams**

Copyright © 2023

All Rights reserved.

No part of this publication may be reproduced,
stored in a retrieval system, or transmitted in any
form or by any means, electronic, mechanical,
photocopying or Otherwise, without the written
permission of the publisher.
The author/editor asserts the moral right to
be identified as the author/editor of this work.

ISBN: 978-93-59324-01-2

Published by

# DOUBLE 9 BOOKS

2/13-B, Ansari Road
Daryaganj, New Delhi – 110002
info@double9books.com
www.double9books.com
Tel. 011-40042856

This book is under public domain

# ABOUT THE AUTHOR

Robert Moore Williams (June 19, 1907 – May 12, 1977) was an American science fiction writer. John S. Browning, H. H. Harmon, Russell Storm, and E. K. Jarvis (a house name) were all pseudonyms. Williams was born in the Missouri town of Farmington. In 1931, he graduated from the Missouri School of Journalism. His first tale, "Zero as a Limit," appeared in Astounding Science Fiction in 1937, under the pen name "Robert Moore." Throughout his career, he was a prolific novelist, with his latest work coming in 1972. His "Jongor" series first appeared in Fantastic Adventures in the 1940s and 1950s, and then in book form in 1970. He had almost 150 pieces published by the 1960s.

# CONTENTS

# CHAPTER I

Jap bombs rained down, there was a tremendous blast—and a weird thing happened to the *Idaho*

The sun came up over a glassy, motionless sea. In the life-boat, Craig arranged the piece of sail to protect them from the sun. He hoisted it to the top of the improvised mast, spreading it so that it threw a shadow on the boat. There was no wind. There had been no wind for three days.

Craig stood up and swept his eyes around the circle of the sea. The horizon was unbroken. As he sat down he was aware that the girl, Margy Sharp, who had been sleeping at his feet, had awakened.

"See anything, pal?" she whispered.

He shook his head.

Her pinched face seemed to become more pinched at his gesture. She sat up. Her eyes went involuntarily to the keg of water beside Craig. She licked her parched, cracked lips.

"How's for a drink, pal?" she asked.

"A quarter of a cup is all we get today," Craig said. "Do you want your share now or will you wait and take it later?"

"I'm terribly thirsty," the girl said. She glanced quickly back at the others in the boat. They were still sleeping.

"How about slipping me a whole cup?" she asked, her bold blue eyes fixed intently on Craig's face.

Craig looked at the sea.

"They're asleep," the girl said quickly. "They won't ever know."

Craig said nothing.

"Please," the girl begged.

Craig sat in silence. He was a big man with a great thatch of black hair and hard gray eyes. He was clad in a pair of torn duck trousers. Rolled bottoms revealed bare feet. He wore no shirt. Holstered on his belt was a heavy pistol.

"Look, big boy," the girl cajoled. "Me and you could get along all right."

"What makes you think so?" Craig questioned.

This was apparently not the answer she had expected. She seemed to be startled. For a moment her eyes measured the man.

"You've been looking for something that you wanted very badly," she said. "You haven't found it. Because you haven't found it, you have become bitter."

Her words made Craig uncomfortable. They came too close to the truth. He shifted his position on the seat.

"So what?" he said.

"So nothing," the girl answered. "Except that we are two of a kind."

"And because we are two of a kind, we can get along?" he questioned.

"Yes," she answered. She made no effort to hide the longing in her eyes. "Look, Craig, me and you, we're tough." She gestured contemptuously at the others in the boat. "*They* aren't tough."

"Aren't they?"

"No." The words came faster now, as if she had made up her mind to say what she had to say and be damned with the consequences. "They're going to die. Oh, you needn't shake your head. You haven't fooled me for a minute with your pretending there will be a ship along to pick us up. There won't be a ship. Our only hope is that we may drift ashore on an island. It may be days before we find an island. There isn't enough water to keep us all alive that long. So—"

She couldn't quite finish what she had to say. Craig watched her, his eyes cold and unrevealing. Her gaze dropped.

"So why don't you and I split the water and let the others die of thirst because we are tough and they aren't? Is that what you mean?" he asked.

"No—" She faltered. "N—no." Defiance hardened her face. "Yes!" she snapped. "That's what I mean. Why should we take care of them? We don't owe them anything. Why should we die with them? What have they—or anybody else—ever done for us? I'll tell you the answer. Nothing. Nothing! *Nothing!*"

"Because they have done nothing for us and because we are the stronger, we let them die. Is that what you mean?"

"Y—yes."

Craig sat in silence for a moment. Dark thoughts were in his mind but his face showed nothing. "I have a gun," he said, "the only gun in the boat. That makes me the boss. Why don't I keep all the water for myself and let the rest of you die of thirst?"

"Oh, you wouldn't do that!" Fright showed on her face.

"Why wouldn't I?" Craig challenged.

"Because—oh, because—"

"What have you got to offer me that is worth a cup of water?" he demanded.

"What have I got that you want?" she answered. Her eyes were fixed hungrily on Craig's face.

"What have you got that I want! Oh, damn it, girl—" The big man twisted uncomfortably. He avoided her gaze, looking instead at the glassy sea.

"Is it time to wake up?" a new voice asked. It was the voice of Mrs. Miller, who had been lying in the middle of the boat. She raised herself to her knees, looked around at the glassy sea. "I thought—" she whispered. "For a moment I thought I was home again. I guess I must have been—dreaming." She pressed her hands against her eyes to shut out the sight of the sea.

"Is it time to have a drink?" she said, looking at Craig.

"No," he said.

"But we always have a drink in the morning," Mrs. Miller protested.

"Not this morning," Craig said.

"May I ask why? Are we—are we out of water?"

"We still have water," Craig answered woodenly.

"Then why can't I have some? I—well, I guess I don't need to tell you why I need a drink."

The reason she needed water was obvious. Worse than anyone else in the boat, Mrs. Miller needed a drink.

"Sorry," Craig shook his head.

"Why?"

"Well, if you must know," Craig said uncomfortably. "Margy and I have decided to keep all the water for ourselves."

"Damn you, Craig!" Margy Sharp said quickly.

"You two have decided—to keep all the—water?" Mrs. Miller said slowly, as if she was trying to understand the meaning of the words. "But what—what about the rest of us?"

"It's too bad for the rest of you," Craig said. He was aware that Margy Sharp was gazing frantically at him but he ignored her. Picking up a tin cup, he held it under the faucet in the side of the keg. A thin stream of water trickled out. He filled the cup half full, and handed it to Margy Sharp.

"Drink up," he said. "Double rations for you and me."

The girl took the cup. She looked at Craig, then glanced quickly at Mrs. Miller. Her parched lips were working but no sound came forth. She looked at the water and Craig could see the movement of her throat as she tried to swallow.

Mrs. Miller said nothing. She stared at Craig and the girl as if she did not understand what she was seeing.

"Damn you, Craig," Margy Sharp said.

"Go on and drink," the big man answered. "That's what you wanted, isn't it?"

"Y—yes."

"Then drink!"

"Oh, damn you—" Tears were in the girl's eyes. While Craig watched woodenly, she turned and crawled back to where Mrs. Miller was sitting.

"Craig was only teasing," she said gently. "He's a great teaser. He meant for you to have the water all the time. Here, Mrs. Miller, this is for you."

"Thank you, dear; thank you ever so much." Mrs. Miller drank the water slowly, in little sips. Margy Sharp watched her. Craig could see the girl trembling. When the last drop was gone, she brought the cup back to Craig—and flung it in his face.

"I could kill you!" she gasped.

"I gave you what you wanted," he said. His voice was impersonal but the hardness had gone from his eyes.

Sobbing, Margy Sharp collapsed in the bottom of the boat. She hid her face in her hands.

"Here," Craig said.

She looked up. He had drawn a fourth of a cup of water and was holding it toward her.

"I—I gave my share to Mrs. Miller," she whispered.

"I know you did," Craig answered. "This is my share."

"But—"

"Water would only rust my stomach," he said. "Take it."

The girl drank. She looked at Craig. There were stars in her eyes.

He leaned forward and patted her on the shoulder. "You'll do, Margy," he said. "You'll do."

The boat floated in the glassy sea. The long ground swell of the Pacific, marching aimlessly toward some unknown shore, lifted it steadily up and down, giving the boat the appearance of moving. An empty tin can, thrown overboard three days previously, floated beside the boat. A school of flying fish, fleeing from some pursuing maw beneath the surface, skipped from wave to wave.

Besides Craig, Margy Sharp, and Mrs. Miller, there were three other persons in the boat, all men. They were: English, a blond youth; Michaelson, a little bird of a man who seemed not yet to have comprehended what had happened to them, or to care; and Voronoff, whose chief distinguishing characteristic was a pair of furtive eyes. English had been wounded. He sat up and looked over the side of the boat. Pointing, he suddenly cried out:

"Look! Look! There's a dragon! A flying dragon!"

"Easy, old man," Craig said gently. For two days English had been delirious. The infection that had developed in his wound was quite beyond the curative powers of the simple medicines carried among the emergency stores of the life boat.

"It's a dragon!" the youth shouted. "It's going to get us."

He stared at something that he could see coming through the air.

Craig drew his pistol. "If it comes after us, I'll shoot it," he said, displaying the gun. "See this pistol."

"That won't stop *this* dragon," English insisted. "Oh—oh—" His eyes widened with fright as he watched something coming through the sky. He ducked down in the bottom of the boat, hid his face in his hands. Men, caught unprotected in the open by a bombing raid, threw themselves to the ground like that, while they waited for the bombs to fall. A few minutes later, English looked up. Relief showed on his face.

"It's gone away," he said. "It flew over and didn't see us."

"There was no danger," Craig said gently. "It wouldn't have harmed us. It was a tame dragon."

"There aren't any tame dragons!" the youth said scornfully. He was looking again at the sea. "There's a snake!" he yelled. "A huge snake! It's got its head out of the water—"

"Poor kid," Margy Sharp whispered. "Can't we do something for him?"

"I'm afraid not," Craig answered. "But you might take him some water." He poured a generous share into the cup, watched the girl take it to the youth, who drank it eagerly.

Michaelson and Voronoff, awakened by the hysterical cries of the youth, were sitting up. Michaelson stared incuriously around him, like a bird that finds itself in a strange forest and wonders how he got there. Then he pulled a small black notebook out of his pocket and began studying it. Ever since he had been in the life boat he had been studying the contents of the notebook, ignoring everything else.

"What's the idea of wasting water on *him*?" Voronoff said sullenly, nodding his head toward English. Margy Sharp was holding the cup to the youth's lips.

"What?" Craig was startled.

"He's done for," Voronoff asserted. He seemed to consider the statement sufficient. He did not attempt to explain it.

A cold glitter appeared in Craig's eyes. "So why waste water on him?" he questioned. "Is that what you mean?"

"That's exactly what I mean," Voronoff answered. "Why waste water on a dead man? We don't have any too much water anyhow."

"Go to hell!" Craig said contemptuously.

"You can say that because you've got the gun," Voronoff said.

Craig's face turned gray with anger but he controlled his temper. "If you think you can taunt me into throwing the gun away, you are mistaken," he said. "In the meantime, I have issued water to everyone else and I assume you and Michaelson will want your shares. If you will come aft, one at a time, I will see that you get it."

"Water?" said Michaelson vaguely. He had paid no attention to the argument. When he heard his name mentioned, he looked up and smiled. "Water? Oh, yes, I believe I would like some." He came aft and Craig held the tin cup under the faucet in the keg. The water rilled out very slowly. Craig stared at it in perplexity. The stream dried to a trickle, then stopped running.

Horror tightened a band around his heart. He lifted the keg, shook it, then set it down.

Michaelson gazed at the few drops of water in the cup. "What is the matter?" he asked. "Is this all I get?"

"The keg is almost empty!" Craig choked out the words.

"Empty?" Michaelson said dazedly. "But yesterday you said it was a quarter full!"

"That was yesterday," Craig said. "Today there isn't over two cups of water left in the keg."

Silence settled over the boat as he spoke. He was aware that four sets of eyes were gazing steadily at him. He picked up the keg, examined it to see if it were leaking. It wasn't. When he set it down, the eyes were still staring at him. There was accusation in them now.

"*You* were the self-appointed guardian of the water supply," Voronoff spat out the words.

Craig didn't answer.

"Last night, when we were asleep, did you help yourself to the water?" Voronoff demanded.

"I did not!" Craig said hotly. "Damn you—"

Voronoff kept silent. Craig looked around the boat. "I don't know what happened to the water," he said. "I didn't drink it, that's certain—"

"Then what became of it?" Michaelson spoke.

He seemed to voice the question in the minds of all the others. If Craig had not taken the water, then what had happened to it? It was gone, the keg didn't leak, and he had been guarding it.

"And here I thought you were a good guy," Margy Sharp said, moving aft.

"Honestly, I didn't drink the water," Craig answered.

"*Honestly?*" she mocked him. "No wonder you were so generous about giving me your share this morning. You had already had all you wanted to drink."

Her voice was bitter and hard.

"If you want to think that, I can't stop you," Craig said.

"I hope you feel good while you stay alive and watch the rest of us die of thirst," the girl said.

"Shut up!"

"I won't shut up. I'll talk all I want to. You won't stop me either. Do you hear that? You won't stop me!"

She was on the verge of hysteria. Craig let her scream. There was nothing he could do to stop her, short of using force. He sat silent and impassive on the seat. Hot fires smouldered behind his eyes. In his mind was a single thought: What had happened to the water?

The boat drifted on the sullen sea. Michaelson, after trying to comprehend what had happened, and failing in the effort, went back to studying the figures in the notebook. Voronoff furtively watched Craig. English had lapsed into a coma. Mrs. Miller huddled in the middle of the boat. She watched the horizon, seeking a sail, a plume of smoke, the sight of a low-lying shore. Margy Sharp had collapsed at Craig's feet. She did not move. Now and then her shoulders jerked as a sob shook her body.

"Well," thought Craig, "I guess this is it. I guess this is the end of the line. I guess this is where we get off. What happens to you after you're dead, I wonder?"

He shrugged. Never in his life had he worried about what would happen after he died and it was too late to begin now.

He was so lost in his thoughts that he did not hear the plane until it had swooped low over them. The roar of its motor jerked his head to the sky. It was an American naval plane, the markings on its wings revealed.

The occupants of the boat leaped to their feet and shouted themselves hoarse. The pilot waggled his wings at them and flew off.

Against the far horizon the superstructure of a warship was visible. It was coming closer. Craig put his fingers to his nose, wiggled them at the sea.

"Damn you, we beat you," he said.

He knew they hadn't beaten the sea. Luck and nothing else had brought that warship near them. Luck had a way of running good for a time. Then it ran bad.

# CHAPTER II
# When the Sun Jumped

"The captain wishes to see you, sir," the sailor said.

Craig snubbed the cigarette and rose to his feet. He had eaten and drank sparingly, very sparingly indeed. They had tried to take him to the hospital bay with the others, but he had gruffly refused. There was nothing wrong with him that a little food and water wouldn't cure.

He followed the sailor to the captain's quarters. Unconsciously he noted the condition of the ship. She was a battleship, the Idaho, one of the new series. Craig guessed she was part of a task force scouting the south Pacific. She was well kept and well manned, he saw. The men went about their tasks with a dash that was heartwarming.

The captain was a tall man. He rose to his feet when Craig entered his quarters, smiled, and held out his hand, "I'm Captain Higgins," he said.

Craig looked at him, blinked, then grinned. He took the out-stretched hand.

"Hi, Stinky," he said. "It's good to see you again."

"Stinky!" Higgins choked. "Sir—"

"Don't get stuffy," Craig said, laughing.

Higgins stared at him. Little by little recognition began to dawn on the captain's face. "Craig!" he whispered. "Winston Craig! This calls for a drink."

"It does, indeed," Craig answered.

Captain Higgins provided the whiskey. It was Scotch. They drank it straight.

"Where on earth have you been?" Higgins asked.

"Gold," Craig said. "Borneo." A frown crossed his face. "Our little brown brothers came down from the north."

"I know," said Higgins grimly. "They came to Pearl Harbor too, the little—. They ran you out of Borneo, eh?"

"I got out," Craig said.

"But this life-boat you were in? What happened?"

"Jap bombers happened. They caught the ship I was on. Luckily we managed to get a few boats away—"

"I see. Where are the other boats?"

"Machine-gunned," Craig said. "A rain squall came along and hid us so they didn't get around to working on the boat I was in." He shrugged. "We were ten days in that boat. I was counting the jewels in the Pearly Gates when your task force came along. But enough about me. What about you?"

Higgins shrugged. "What you can see," he said.

Craig nodded. He could see plenty. The boy who had been known as "Stinky" in their days at Annapolis was boss of a battle wagon.

"I heard you resigned your commission within a year after we had finished at the Academy," Higgins said.

"Yes," Craig answered.

"Mind if I ask why?"

"Not at all. I just wanted some action and it didn't look as if I could get it in the Navy. So—"

It was not so much what Craig said as what he left unsaid that was important. He was a graduate of the Naval Academy at Annapolis. He and Stinky Higgins had finished in the same class. Higgins had stayed with the Navy. Craig had not been able to endure the inactivity of belonging to a fighting organization when there was no fighting to be done. He was born with the wanderlust, with itching feet, with the urge to see what lay beyond the farthermost horizon.

"So you were prospecting for gold?" Captain Higgins asked.

"Yes."

"What are you going to do now, if I may ask?"

"Well," Craig said, "I was on my way back to the States, to join up again, if they would take me."

Higgins grinned. "If they would take you? They will grab you with open arms. They could use a million like you."

"Thanks," Craig said.

A knock sounded on the door.

"What is it?" Higgins said to the aide who entered.

"One of the men we picked up in the life-boat wants to see you, sir."

"What about?"

"He would not say, sir. He insists it is of the utmost importance. His name is Michaelson, sir. Shall I show him to your quarters?"

"Very well. I'll see him immediately."

The aide saluted smartly and left.

"Who is this Michaelson?" Higgins said to Craig.

"I don't know," Craig shrugged. "Just one of the passengers in the life-boat. We didn't ask each other for pedigrees. About all I can say about him is that he is a queer duck." Craig explained how Michaelson had been constantly studying the contents of the notebook he carried.

The captain frowned. "There is a Michaelson who is a world-famous scientist," he said. "I don't suppose this could be he."

"Might be," Craig said. "This is the south seas. You never know who is going to turn up down here or what is going to happen." Abruptly he stopped speaking. A new sound was flooding through the ship.

It had been years since he had heard that sound yet he recognized it instantly. The call to action stations! It could have only one meaning. The Idaho was going into action. Something thrilled through Craig's blood at the thought. He turned questioning eyes toward the captain.

Higgins was already on the phone.

"Flight of Jap bombers approaching," he said, flinging the phone back on its hook. "Come on."

This was probably the first time in naval history that a bare-footed, bare-headed man, whose sole articles of clothing consisted of a pair of dirty duck trousers, joined the commanding officer of a battleship on the captain's bridge. Captain Higgins didn't care what Craig was wearing, and his officers, if they cared, were too polite to show it. They didn't really care anyhow. They had other things on their minds.

Far off in the sky Craig could see what the officers had on their minds. A series of tiny black dots. They were so far away they looked like gnats. Jap bombers. Big fellows. Four-engined jobs.

The notes of the call to action stations were still screaming through the ship. The Idaho, at the touch of the magic sound, was coming to life. Thirty-five thousand tons of steel was going into action. Craig could feel the pulsation as the engines kicked the screws over faster. The ship surged ahead. Fifteen hundred men were leaping to their stations. The guns in the big turrets were poking around, hoping that somewhere off toward the horizon there was a target for them. The Idaho was a new ship. She was lousy with anti-aircraft. The black muzzles of multiple pom-poms were swinging around, poking toward the sky.

An officer was peering through a pair of glasses. "Seventeen of them, sir," he said. "I can't be certain yet, but I think there is another flight following the first."

The Idaho was part of a task force that included a carrier, cruisers, and several destroyers. Craig could see the carrier off in the distance. She had already swung around. Black gnats were racing along her deck and leaping into the sky. Fighter planes going up. Cruisers and destroyers were moving into pre-determined positions around the carrier and the Idaho, to add the weight of their anti-aircraft barrage to the guns carried by the big ships.

"Three minutes," somebody said in a calm voice. "They've started on their run."

The anti-aircraft let go. Craig gasped and clamped his hands over his ears. He had left the Navy before the advent of air warfare. He knew the roar of the big guns in their turrets but this was his first experience with the guns that fought the planes. The sound was utterly deafening. If the fury of a hundred thunder-storms were concentrated into a single area, the blasting tornado of sound would not be as great as the thunder of the guns. The explosions beat against his skull, set his teeth pounding together. He could feel the vibrations with his feet.

High in the sky overhead black dots blossomed like death flowers blooming in the sky.

The bombers kept coming.

The anti-aircraft bursts moved into their path. Death reached up into the sky, plucking with taloned fingers for the black vultures racing with the wind. Reached and found their goal. One plane mushroomed outward in a burst of smoke.

Craig knew it was a direct hit, apparently in the bomb bay, exploding the bombs carried there. Fragments of the plane hung in the sky, falling slowly downward.

Up above the anti-aircraft, midges were dancing in the sun—fighter planes. They dived downward.

Abruptly a bomber fell out of formation, tried to right itself, failed. A wing came off. Crazily the bomber began spinning.

Black smoke gouted from a third ship. It began losing altitude rapidly.

The others continued on their course.

Michaelson suddenly appeared on the bridge.

How he got there, Craig did not know, but he was there, jumping around and waving his notebook in the air. Michaelson was shouting at the top of his voice.

"—Danger!—Must get away from here—"

Craig caught the shouted words. The thundering roar of the anti-aircraft barrage drowned out the rest.

No one paid any attention to Michaelson. They were watching the sky.

The planes had released their bombs.

For some reason they were not attacking their normal target, the carrier. Perhaps a second flight was making a run over the carrier. The first flight was bombing the battleship.

The Idaho was their target.

Craig could feel the great ship tremble as she tried to swerve to avoid the bombs. A destroyer would have been able to spin in a circle but 35,000 tons of steel do not turn so easily.

The bombs were coming down. Craig could see them in the air, little black dots growing constantly larger. Fighter planes were tearing great holes in the formation of the bombers. Few of the Jap ships would ever return to their base. But their job was already done.

The bombs hit.

They struck in an irregular pattern all around the ship. Four or five were very near misses but there was not one direct hit. Great waterspouts leaped from the surface of the sea. A sheet of flame seemed to run around the horizon. It was a queer, dancing, intensely brilliant, blue flame. It looked like the discharge from some huge electric arc.

Even above the roar of the barrage, Craig heard the tearing sound. Somehow it reminded him of somebody tearing a piece of cloth. Only, to make a sound as loud as this, it would have to be a huge piece of cloth and the person tearing it would have to be a giant.

The blue light became more intense. It flared to a brilliance that was intolerable.

At the same time, the sun jumped!

"I'm going nuts!" the fleeting thought was in Craig's mind. He wondered if a bomb had struck the ship. Was this the nightmare that comes with death?

Had he died in the split fraction of a second and was his disintegrating mind reporting the startling fact of death by telling him that the sun was jumping?

The sun couldn't jump.

It *had* jumped. It had been almost directly overhead. Now it was two hours down the western sky.

Tons of water were cascading over the bow of the ship. Waves were leaping over the deck. The Idaho seemed to have sunk several feet. Now her buoyancy was asserting itself and she was trying to rise out of the sea. She was fighting her way upward, rising against the weight of the water.

A wind was blowing. There had been almost no wind but now a gale of hurricane proportions was howling through the superstructure of the ship.

A heavy sea was running. The sea had been glassy smooth. Now it was covered with white caps.

The bombs had exploded, a blue light had flamed, a giant had ripped the sky apart, a gale had leaped into existence, the sea had covered itself with white capped waves, and the sun had jumped.

Craig looked at the sky, seeking the second flight of bombers. The air was filled with scudding clouds. There were no bombers in sight.

The anti-aircraft batteries, with no target, suddenly stopped firing.

Except for the howl of the wind through the superstructure, the ship was silent. The silence was so heavy it hurt the ears. The officers on the bridge stood without moving, frozen statues. They seemed paralyzed.

The ship was running herself.

"W—what—what the hell became of those Jappos?" Craig heard a dazed officer say.

"Yeah, what happened to those bombers?"

"Where did this wind come from?"

"There wasn't any wind a minute ago."

"Look at the sea. It's covered with white caps!"

"Something happened to the sun. I—I'm almost positive I saw it move."

Dazed, bewildered voices.

"What the devil became of the carrier?" That was the voice of Captain Higgins.

"And the rest of the force, the cruisers and destroyers—what became of them?"

Craig looked toward the spot where he had last seen the carrier. She had been launching planes.

He did not believe his eyes.

The carrier was gone.

The cruisers and destroyers that had been cutting foaming circles around the carrier and the battleship—were gone.

The surface of the sea was empty. There weren't even any puffs of exploding shells in the sky.

The Idaho plunged forward through strange seas. From horizon to horizon there was nothing to be seen. The task force to which the ship belonged and the attacking Jap planes had both vanished. The group of officers responsible for the ship were dazed. Then, little by little, their long training asserted itself and they fought off the panic threatening them. Captain Higgins ordered the ship slowed until she was barely moving. This was to protect them from the possibility of hitting submerged reefs or shoals. The first question was—what had happened? Captain Higgins ordered radio silence broken. The ship carried powerful wireless equipment, strong enough to reach to the mainland of America, and farther.

The radio calls brought no response. The radio men reported all they could get on their receivers was static. No commercial and no radio signals were on the air. This was impossible.

In growing bewilderment, Captain Higgins ordered a plane catapulted into the air, to search the surrounding sea. Meanwhile routine reports from all parts of the ship showed that the Idaho had suffered no damage of any kind from the bombing. She was in first-class shape. The only thing wrong with her was the men who manned her. They were bewildered. Defeat in battle they would have faced. They would not have flinched if the ship had gone down before superior gun power. They would have fought her fearlessly, dying, if need be, in the traditions of their service.

Craig was still on the bridge with Captain Higgins and the other officers. Although he did not show it, he was scared. Right down to the bottoms of his bare feet, he was scared. He watched the scouting plane catapulted into the air, and the grim thought came into his mind that Noah, sending forth the dove from the ark, must have been in a similar position. Like Noah, Captain Higgins was sending forth a dove to search the waste of waters.

Besides Craig, there was another civilian on the bridge, Michaelson. Nobody was paying any attention to him. Normally, if he had intruded without invitation to this sacred spot, he would have been bounced off so fast it would have made his head swim. But the officers had other things to think about besides a stray civilian who had popped out of nowhere. Michaelson, after fluttering vainly from officer to officer and getting no attention, turned at last to Craig. Michaelson was waving his note book.

"These men will pay no attention to me," Michaelson complained, nodding toward the officers.

"They got troubles," Craig said. "They've run into a problem that is driving them nuts."

"But I could help them solve their problem!" Michaelson said, irritation in his voice.

"Aw, beat it—Huh? What did you say?" Craig demanded.

"I can tell them what happened, if they will only listen. I was trying to warn them, before it happened, but I was unable to reach the bridge in time."

"You—*you know what happened*?" Craig choked.

"Certainly!" Michaelson said emphatically.

Craig stared at the little man. Michaelson did not look like he had much on the ball but he spoke excellent English, and even if he was a queer duck, he seemed to be intelligent. Craig remembered that Michaelson had been trying to reach the bridge just before the bombers struck, also that the man had been trying to get in touch with the captain just before the warning sounded that the bombers were approaching. Craig turned to the officers.

"Captain Higgins," he said.

"Don't bother me now, Craig," the captain snapped.

"There's a man here who wants to talk to you," Craig said.

"I have no time—" For the first time, the captain saw Michaelson. "Who the devil are you?" he snapped. "What are you doing on my bridge?"

"He's the man who wants to talk to you," Craig explained. "His name is Michaelson."

Michaelson smiled shyly. "You may have heard of me," he said.

"Are you Michaelson the scientist, the man who is called the second Einstein?" Higgins demanded.

Michaelson blushed. "I am a scientist," he said. "As for being a second Einstein, no. There is only one Einstein. There can be only one. But it may be that I can help you with your problem."

Craig saw the attitude of the officers change. They had heard of Michaelson. It was a great name. Until then they had not known that he was on their bridge. They became respectful.

"If you can help us, shoot," Higgins said bluntly.

"I will try," the scientist said. He pursed his lips and looked thoughtful. "If you are familiar with geology you unquestionably know something about 'faults'. 'Faults' are unstable areas on the surface of the earth, places where, due to joints or cracks in the underlying strata of rocks, slippage is likely to take place. There is, for instance, the great San Andreas Rift, in California, which is a 'fault'."

"Sorry, Mr. Michaelson," Higgins interrupted. "If you've got something to say, say it, but don't start giving us a lecture on geology."

"In explaining the unknown, it is best to start with what is known," the scientist answered. "Earth faults are known. When I talk about them, you will understand me. However, there is another kind of fault that is as yet unknown, or known only to a few scientists who suspected its existence—" He paused. "I am referring to the space-time fault."

The faces of the officers registered nothing. Craig frowned, but listened with quickened interest. A space-time fault! What was Michaelson talking about?

"You will not find a space-time fault mentioned in any scientific treatise," Michaelson continued. "There is no literature on the subject, as yet. Certain erratic phenomena, of which the apparent slowing of the speed of light in certain earth areas was the most important, led a few scientists to speculate on the existence of some strange condition of space and time that would account for the observed phenomena. The speed of light is regarded as being constant, yet in certain places on earth, for no apparent reason, light seemed to move slower than it did elsewhere. What was the reason for this strange slow-down? Investigation revealed the existence of what I have called a space-time fault."

"Please, Mr. Michaelson," Captain Higgins spoke. "We are not scientists. With all respect to your ability, I must request you to come directly to the point."

"Very well," the scientist said. "We have fallen into a space-time fault. I have been conducting certain researches in and near this area in an effort to locate the boundaries of what I had hoped would be called—since I discovered it—the Michaelson Fault. Under ordinary circumstances the ship would, in all probability, have passed directly through the fault, though I suspect, from certain data of ships that have disappeared mysteriously, that *all* ships have not always passed through the fault. In our case, the explosion of the bombs was sufficient to cause a momentary dislodgment of the space-time balance in this area, with the result that we were precipitated through the fault."

He paused and looked expectantly at his audience. It was his impression that he had made a complete explanation of what had happened. He expected the officers to understand. They didn't understand.

Craig, watching in silence, caught a vague glimpse of what the scientist was saying. He felt a cold chill run up and down his spine. If he understood Michaelson correctly—

"We were precipitated through the fault?" a lieutenant spoke. "I don't follow. What do you mean, sir?"

"Mean?" Michaelson answered. "I mean we passed through the fault."

"But what does that mean?"

"That we have passed through time!"

Craig was aware of a mounting tension when he heard the words. Then he had understood Michaelson correctly! He had been afraid of that. He saw from the faces of the officers that they either did not comprehend what the scientist had said, or comprehending, were refusing to believe.

"Passed through time!" somebody said. "But that is ridiculous."

Michaelson shrugged. "You are thinking with your emotions," he said. "You are thinking wishfully. You hope we have not passed through time. Therefore you say it is not true."

"But," Captain Higgins spoke, "if we have passed through time, how far have we gone, and in what direction?"

"How far I cannot say," Michaelson answered. "There is little question of the direction: We have gone back. A space-time fault can only slip back. It cannot slip forward, or I cannot conceive of it slipping forward. As to the distance we have gone, in space, a few feet. In time, the distance may be a hundred thousand years. It may be a million years, or ten million." He tapped his notebook. "I have much data here, but not enough data to determine how far we have gone."

Craig was cold, colder than he had ever been in all his life. They had passed through time! Desperately he wanted to doubt that the scientist knew what he was talking about. His eyes sought the reassurance of the battleship. Surely such a mass of steel could not pass through time! But— the sun had jumped, a hurricane of wind had roared out of nowhere and was still roaring through the rigging of the ship. The calm sea had become storm-tossed. And—the radio was silent.

Was Michaelson right? Or was he a madman? Craig could not grasp completely the reasoning of the scientist. A space-time fault sounded impossible. But there was no question about the existence of earth faults. Craig had seen a few of those areas where the foundations of the earth had crumpled. If the inconceivable pressures of the planet could crush miles of rock like he could crush a playing card in his hands, why could not the more tenuous fabric of space-time be crushed also?

The faces of the officers reflected doubt. Craig saw them steal uneasy glances at each other, saw them glance at the bulk of the battleship for reassurance. The ship was their world.

Out of the corner of his eyes Craig saw something coming across the sea. At the same time, in the forepeak, a lookout sang out.

"I'm afraid," Craig said, pointing, "that now there is no doubt that Mr. Michaelson is right. Look there."

Sailing down the wind was a gigantic bird-lizard. With great fanged beak out-stretched, it was flapping through the air on leathery wings. It was a creature out of the dawn of time.

It proved, by its mere existence, that Michaelson was right.

The Idaho, and all her crew, had passed through a space-time fault into an antediluvian world!

# CHAPTER III
# The Return of the Dove

There were dozens of the great bird-lizards flapping about the ship. Either they thought it was an enemy, to be attacked and destroyed, or they thought it was something to eat. In either event, it was to be attacked. They were attacking it. They would circle it, flap heavily to a point above, then launch themselves into a glide, fanged mouth open, screaming shrilly.

The anti-aircraft gunners knocked the beasts out of the air with ease.

On the bridge a group of tense officers watched the slaughter without being greatly interested in it. They knew that the guns of the Idaho were proof against any creature of earth, sky, or water, in this world. They were not afraid of the beasts of this strange time into which they had been thrust.

The scouting plane was still out, searching the waste of water for land.

The officers of the Idaho were all thinking the same thing. Captain Higgins put their thoughts into words.

"Mr. Michaelson," the captain said slowly. "I can't argue with you. I am forced to believe that somehow we have been forced back in time. However I am charged with the responsibility for this ship. Back where we came from, the Idaho is needed. I want to get her back where she belongs. How can we accomplish this?"

The scientist hesitated. He did not want to say what he had to say. He shook his head. "I question whether or not we can accomplish it," he said at last.

"But we *have* to return!" Higgins protested.

"I know," Michaelson said sympathetically. "The problem is *how*!"

"You mean there is no way to return?"

The scientist shrugged. "If there is, I do not know of it."

"But can't you make any suggestion? After all, this is your field. You're a scientist."

"This is my field but even I know little or nothing about it. Almost nothing is known about the true nature of the space-time continuum. Only recently have we even guessed that such things as space-time faults existed. We were hurled through this particular fault by accident, the result of an unfortunate combination of circumstances. Whether we can duplicate that accident, and whether it would return us to our own time—I just don't know. Nobody knows."

The officers of the Idaho received this information with no sign of pleasure. Craig felt sorry for them. After all, some of them had wives, all of them had friends back in the United States. Or was it *forward* in the United States, in the America that was to be? It was hard to remember that Columbus had not as yet sailed westward, would not sail westward for—how many hundreds of thousands of years?

All human history would have to unroll before there was an America. If the theory of continental drift was correct, there might not even be an American continent, it might still be joined to Europe. Babylon and Nineveh, Karnak and Thebes, Rome and London—there were no such cities in the world, would not be for—

The men on this ship were probably the only human beings alive on earth! Men had not yet become human, or maybe hadn't. The Neanderthal Man, the Cro-Magnons, maybe the Java Man, the Piltdown Man, had not yet appeared on the planet!

"As I understand it," an officer said, "we were sailing directly across a space-time fault when the explosion of the bombs sent us through the fault? Is that correct?"

"That is correct," Michaelson answered.

"Then why don't we locate this fault and set off some explosions of our own?" the officer suggested. "Is there any chance that we might return—home—that way?"

"I don't know," the scientist frankly answered. "Maybe it would work, maybe it won't. We can certainly try it, and if it fails, nothing is lost. Meanwhile I will go over my data and see if I can find some way of accomplishing what we desire."

Michaelson went below. The Idaho was brought around. Immediately a worried officer posed another problem.

"How are we going to find that fault?" he asked. "We can't see it. We can't feel it. How are we going to know when we have reached the right place?"

"We'll search the whole area," Higgins said. "We haven't moved far and locating the fault ought not to be too difficult. For that matter, we are probably still in it."

The officers moved quickly and efficiently to put his orders into execution. The plan was to put the ship in the same position she had occupied when the bombs struck, then use the small boats to plant explosive charges in the water around the battle wagon, charges which could be electrically exploded from the ship. Captain Higgins moved to where Craig was standing. He took off his cap and wiped perspiration from his forehead.

"What do you make of this?" he asked.

Craig shrugged. "I pass," he said.

"But—one minute we were part of a task force and Jap bombers were having a go at us. The next minute—" Higgins looked helpless. "Damn it, Craig," he exploded, "things like that can't happen!"

"They aren't supposed to happen," the big man grimly answered. "We just saw one of them happen."

"But—" Higgins protested, "surely we would have known about these space-time faults, if they existed. Other ships would have fallen into them."

"Maybe other ships have fallen into them," Craig suggested. "In the last war the Cyclops vanished without a trace. There have been other ships, dozens of them, that have disappeared. And, for that matter, how is the commander of your task force going to handle the disappearance of the Idaho?"

"I don't know," Higgins muttered.

"He is going to have to report the loss of the battleship. What will he say?"

"What can he say?"

"He'll search the area, for survivors and wreckage. When he finds neither the only conclusion he can reach will be that the Idaho was instantaneously sunk with the loss of all hands. Remember we were under attack at the time. Remember that intense blue light that flared around the horizon? To the men in the other ships that light may have looked like an explosion of the magazines of the Idaho. The admiral commanding your task force may report that a bomb seemingly passed down the smoke stack of the Idaho and the resulting explosion touched off the powder magazine."

Craig paused and in growing perplexity watched what Higgins was doing. The captain was vigorously kicking the steel wall of the bridge. He was pounding his right foot against it as if he was trying to kick it down. There was a look of pain on his face. Craig watched for a second, then grinned.

"Does it hurt?" he said.

"Yes!"

"Then it must be real," the big man suggested.

Higgins left off kicking the wall. Craig knew *why* he had been kicking it—to assure himself that the wall was really there. Higgins was a man in a nightmare but instead of pinching himself to see if he was awake, he kicked the wall.

"Damn it!" the captain muttered. "Why did this have to happen to us?"

"Destiny," Craig mused. "Fate. How did the steamer I was on happen to get bombed? How did I happen to be in the life-boat that wasn't machine-gunned? How did we happen to get picked up? The only answer is fate."

"That's a darned poor answer," Higgins said.

"It's the only answer," Craig replied. "Your dove is coming back."

"What? Have you gone wacky on me?" the startled captain answered.

Craig pointed to the sea. Barely visible on the horizon was a tiny dot.

"Oh, the plane," the captain said, watching the dot. It was moving swiftly toward them.

Craig watched it, a frown on his face. "I thought you sent out only *one* plane," he said.

"That's right. I did send one."

"Well," Craig said slowly, "unless my eyes have gone bad, three planes are coming back."

"What?—But that's impossible?" Higgins snatched a pair of glasses, swiftly focused them on the plane. It was still only a dot in the sky. Two smaller dots were following swiftly behind it.

"Maybe a couple of those lizard-birds are chasing it?" Craig hazarded.

"Nonsense!" the captain retorted. "It can fly rings around those things. Those lizards are too slow to keep up with it. But there is something following it."

Higgins kept the glasses to his eyes, straining to see the approaching dots.

"If those things are planes," he muttered, and there was a note of exultation in his voice, "then Michaelson, and his talk of space-time faults, is nuts."

What Higgins meant was, that if the two dots were planes, then what had happened to the Idaho had been an illusion of some kind. Planes could exist only in a modern world. They were one of mankind's most recent inventions.

The stubby-winged scouting plane from the ship was easily visible now. It was driving hell for leather for the Idaho. Craig watched it with growing apprehension.

"That pilot is running away from something," he said.

"Impossible!" Higgins snapped.

The plane swept nearer. It was flying at a low altitude. The two dots were hard on its heels. They were overtaking it. And—they were no longer dots.

"Planes!" Higgins shouted.

Craig kept silent. They were planes all right, but—He saw something lance out from one of them. The scouting plane leaped upward in a screaming climb. Something reached toward it again, touched it. It began to lose altitude. It was still coming toward the Idaho but it was on a long slant.

"It's being attacked!" Higgins shouted, pain in his voice.

Over the Idaho the call to battle stations rolled. Again the mighty vessel surged to the tempo of men going into action.

The scouting plane was dropping lower and lower. It hit the water. One of the pursuing ships dived down at it.

The anti-aircraft batteries let go. For the second time the Idaho was defending herself. Thunder rolled across the waters.

The attacking plane was within point-blank range. Mushrooms of black smoke puffed into existence around it, knocked it around in the air, caught it with a direct hit.

A gigantic explosion sounded.

A ball of smoke burst where the plane had been. Fragments floated outward, slid downward to the sea. There was not enough of the plane left for identification.

The second plane lifted upward. For the first time Craig got a good look at it. His first impression, illogical as that was, was that it was a Jap ship.

When it lifted up he got a good look at it. It wasn't a Jap plane. No marks of the rising sun were visible on its body.

Craig saw then that it wasn't a plane at all. It had stubby, sloping wings, but the wings were apparently more for the purpose of stabilizing flight than for the lift they might impart. It looked like a flying wedge.

He could not tell how it was propelled. If it had a motor, he could not see it.

It was fast, faster than greased lightning.

Apparently its pilot had not noticed the battleship until the barrage of anti-aircraft fire had destroyed the first plane. Not until then did he even know the Idaho existed. Like a bird that had been suddenly startled by the appearance of a hawk, the plane leaped into the air. Shells were still bursting around it. It went up so fast it left the barrage completely behind. Its climb was almost vertical. It rose to about twenty thousand feet, leveled off. Twice it circled the battleship, ignoring the shell bursts, that tried to keep up with it.

Then it turned in the direction from which it had come. It was out of sight in seconds.

There was silence on the bridge of the Idaho.

"Holy cats!" Craig heard an officer mutter. "Somebody is crazy as hell. *We* don't have planes that will fly like that and I know damned good and well they didn't have them a hundred thousand years ago!"

Was Michaelson wrong? Was he talking through his hat when he said the Idaho had been precipitated through a time fault into the remote past? He had said they might be a hundred thousand years in the past, or a million years—he didn't know which. The appearance of the lizard-birds, the great winged dragons of mythology, had seemed to prove that the scientist was correct.

Did these two mysterious planes, of strange shape and design and with the ability to fly at such blinding speed, prove that he was wrong?

Was it possible—the thought stunned Craig—that they had been precipitated into the future?

The winged dragons belonged to the past. The planes, theoretically at least, belonged to the future.

"Something is crazy!" Captain Higgins said. "Go get that scientist," he spoke to one of his aides. "I want to talk to him."

Michaelson came to the bridge and listened quietly to what Higgins had to say. His grave face registered no emotion but his eyes were grim.

"I can definitely tell you *two* things," he said at last. "One of them is that we are not in what could be called the future."

"But those two planes were better than anything we have invented!" Captain Higgins insisted. "The airplane was not invented until 1907. This *has* to be the future."

"*Men* invented airplanes in 1907," Michaelson said. Ever so slightly he emphasized the word "*men*."

Higgins stared at him. Slowly, as he realized the implication of what the scientist had said, his face began to change. "What are you driving at?" he said, his voice a whisper.

Michaelson spread his hands in a helpless gesture. "The Wright brothers invented the lighter-than-air ship early in the twentieth century," he said. "They were the first men to fly a plane, the first men of our race. But how do we know what happened on earth a million years ago, and I can definitely tell you that we are at least a million years in the past? The history that we know fairly well does not cover a span of more than five thousand years. How can we be certain what happened or did not happen on earth millions of years ago?"

The scientist spoke quietly, his voice almost a whisper. "We are before the time of the airplane. Yet we find airplanes? What do you think that might mean?"

"I—" Higgins faltered, his mind flinching away from facing the unknown gulfs of time. He forced his mind to heel. "It means there are people here in this time," he said huskily. "People, or *something*, who know how to make planes."

Michaelson nodded. "That would be my conclusion," he said.

"But that is impossible," Higgins flared. "If there had been civilizations in the past, we would have a record of them. I mean, we would have found their cities, even if the people had disappeared. We would have found traces of their factories, of their buildings—"

"Would we?" Michaelson asked.

"Certainly. Don't you agree with me?"

"Not necessarily," the scientist said. "You are forgetting one important fact—the size of a million years. A million years from now will anyone be able to find New York? Chicago? London? The steel mills of Pittsburgh?

I think not. In that length of time, the action of the rain, the frost, and the sun will have completely destroyed every sign that these places once existed. Besides, the continents we now know may have sunk and new ones appeared. How could we locate the ruin of Pittsburgh if the city were at the bottom of the Atlantic? A million years ago there may have been huge cities on earth. Man is not necessarily the first race ever to appear on the planet."

Craig, listening, recognized the logic in what Michaelson had said. There might have been other races on earth! The vanity of men blinded them to that fact, when they thought about it at all. They wanted to believe they were the most important, and the only effort of creation, that the earth had come into being expressly for their benefit. Nature might have other plans.

Michaelson had suggested a logical solution for the dilemma of airplanes and flying dragons existing in the same world.

Craig saw the officers glancing uneasily in the direction from which the planes had come. Off yonder somewhere below the horizon was *something*. They were worried about it. Against the beasts of this time, the Idaho was all-powerful. But how would the Idaho stack up against the *something* that lay below the horizon? Or would the ship be able to escape back through the time fault before the threat of the mysterious planes became greater?

Out around the ship, small boats were planting charges of explosive. One boat was dashing out to the wrecked scouting plane to rescue the pilot.

"We have to see if we can get away from here, at once," Higgins said. "We have to set off those explosives and see if they will force us back through the time fault."

They had to get away from this world. There was danger here. Planes that flew as fast as the one that had gone streaking off across the sky represented danger.

Higgins ordered the planting of the explosives to proceed at the double-quick.

"I said I could definitely tell you two things," Michaelson spoke again. "One of them was that we are in the past, millions of years in the past." He spoke slowly, his eyes on the busy boats around the ship. "Are you not interested in the second of the two things I said I could tell you?"

"Yes," said Higgins. "What is it?"

The scientist sighed. "It is that we will never be able to return to our own time!"

"What? But—we are planting mines. If the explosion of the Jap bombs sent us through the time fault, maybe a second explosion will send us back through it."

Michaelson shook his head. "I have investigated the mathematics of it," he said. "It is impossible. You might as well call in your boats and save your explosives. The fact is, we are marooned in this time, *forever!*"

Marooned in time, forever! The words rang like bells of doom. Marooned forever. No chance of escape. No hope for escape.

"Are you sure?" Higgins questioned.

"Positive," the scientist answered.

Craig looked at the sea. He lit a cigarette, noting that it was the last one in the package. He drew the smoke into his lungs, feeling the bite of it.

Marooned in time, forever!

# CHAPTER IV
## Silver on the Sea

Night had come hours ago. Craig stood on the deck, watching the sea and the sky and the stars in the sky. Up overhead the constellations had changed. They were not the familiar star clusters that he knew. Completely blacked out, the Idaho moved very slowly through the darkness. Her speed was kept to almost nothing because the charts of the navigators were useless. The charts had been made in that far future which the battle wagon had quitted forever and they revealed nothing about this sea. There might be a mile of water under the ship. She might be scraping bottom. The navigators were going mad worrying about what might be under the ship. Captain Higgins was going mad worrying not only about what might be under the ship but about what might soon be over it, when the mysterious planes returned. The pilot of the scouting plane had been rescued. He had not lived to tell what he had found.

Craig was aware of a shadow near him but he thought it was one of the crew until the match flared. It was Margy Sharp. She was lighting a cigarette.

A sharp reprimand from an officer caused her to drop the match.

"What's wrong?" she demanded. "Why can't I smoke?"

"Blackout," Craig said.

"Oh, it's *you*," the girl spoke.

"Where have you been?" Craig asked. "I looked around for you but I couldn't find you."

"In the hospital," she said. "Helping out a baffled doctor."

"How is English?" Craig asked.

"English has been dead for hours," she said. "I've been with Mrs. Miller."

"Oh! How is she?"

"Fine. But the doctor almost went nuts. He said it was the first time in naval history that a baby had been born on a battleship. He seemed to think it violated the rules of etiquette, or something. It was a girl," she went on, a little breathlessly now, as if talking about babies made her excited. "Mrs. Miller said she was going to name it Margaret, after me. Isn't that nice? She says her husband will be worried to death about her and she wants to use the ship's radio to send him a message. Do you think she could do that?"

"Do I—" Craig choked. "Listen, girl, do you know what has happened?"

The tone of his voice alarmed her. "No," she said quickly. "I don't know. What has happened?"

She had been busy down in the hospital bay, too busy to wonder what was going on up above. Craig told her the whole story. She listened in incredulous amazement. He had to tell it twice before she began to understand it. And then she didn't believe it.

"You're kidding me," she said.

"Sorry," Craig answered. "But I'm not kidding."

"You mean—you actually mean we're back somewhere in the past?"

"Exactly."

"But—but what are we going to do?"

The big man shrugged. "We're going to wait and see what happens. That's all we can do. Wait and see." There were tones of excitement in his voice.

"You sound pleased about this," she challenged.

"I'm not pleased," he quickly corrected her. "I'm sorry for Mrs. Miller and for Margaret, for you, for Captain Higgins, and the men on the Idaho. But as for myself—well, I'm not sorry. This is the ultimate adventure. We have a new world to explore, new things to see. I know hundreds of men who would give an arm to be dropped back here into this world. I've met them in every mining camp I ever saw, in every trading post on the frontiers of civilization, in every corner of earth. They were misfits, most of them. I'm a misfit, or I was, back in our time. I didn't belong, I didn't fit in. I wasn't a business man, I never would have made a business man. I couldn't have been a lawyer or a clerk or a white-collar worker. But here—well I seem to belong here. This is my time, this is my place in the world." He broke off. "I don't know why I am telling you all this," he said shortly.

She had listened quietly and sympathetically. "You can tell me," she said. "Remember, back in the life-boat, when I told you we were two of a kind? I didn't fit in, either, back home. I belong here too."

She had moved closer to him, in the soft darkness. He could sense her nearness, sense her womanliness. He started to put his arms around her.

"Well," a voice said behind him.

Craig turned. Voronoff stood there. "What do you want?" Craig said.

"From you, I want nothing," Voronoff answered. "I was not speaking to you. I, at least, have not forgotten about the water."

"The water?" Craig said puzzled. "What are you talking about?"

"The water that wasn't in the cask we had in the life-boat," Voronoff answered. "The water that you drank in the night when the rest of us were asleep."

"Damn you—" Craig said.

Voronoff walked away. Craig made no attempt to follow him. He had completely forgotten about the water. With an effort, he got his temper under control and turned back to the girl.

She had turned away and was looking at the sea. When Craig spoke, she did not answer. A moment before, a warm magic had been between them. Voronoff's words had changed the warmth to coldness.

That night the lookouts on the Idaho were constantly reporting that the ship was being shadowed. Overhead in the darkness were planes, silent planes. The lookout occasionally spotted them against the moon.

The fact that the planes flew silently, like shadows in the night, perturbed the lookouts and their uneasiness was communicated to the crew. No one would have much minded planes that made the proper amount of noise, but ghost planes that made no noise at all were dreadful things. The silent planes scouted the ship, then seemed to disappear. At least they were no longer visible, but whether or not they were still hidden somewhere in the sky, no one knew. They made no attempt to bomb the ship, or to attack it in any way. This seemed ominous.

The Idaho carried four planes of her own. One had been lost. Before dawn, Captain Higgins ordered another catapulted into the sky, to search the surrounding area. This plane went aloft. It was not attacked or molested. The pilot, by radio, reported the presence of a large body of land very near. Navigators, consulting their charts, discovered that this body of land was not on any of their maps.

Dawn, that hour of danger when an attack might reasonably be expected, came. The crew of the Idaho stood by their guns, waiting. No attack came.

The sun rose. Still there was no attack. The ship, moving very slowly, entered an area where the surface of the sea seemed to have turned to silver. This effect was caused by some oily substance that floated on the water, a new phenomenon to officers and men alike.

On the horizon the land mass the pilot of the scouting plane had reported was dimly visible, a range of forested hills sloping upward to mountains in the background, the rim of some mighty continent of the old time. Later, millions of years later, only the tops of these mountains would remain above the sea, to form the thousands of islands of the Pacific.

Craig breakfasted below. He came on deck just as the alarm sounded. The crew raced to their stations. He discovered the cause of the alarm.

Overhead, at a height of thirty to thirty-five thousand feet, was a plane. It was shadowing the ship. It made no attempt to attack. Craig went to the bridge. Captain Higgins had been on the bridge all night. He was still there. He greeted Craig wanly.

"We're being watched," Higgins said. "I don't like it."

"Anything we can do about it?"

Higgins squinted upward through his glasses. "Too high for ack-ack. No, there is nothing we can do about it. And I'm not sure we want to do anything about it."

"What do you mean?"

"We're not fighting a war here in *this* time," the captain answered. "We don't want to fight, if we can possibly avoid it."

"It may be a problem to avoid fighting," Craig said. "Remember, they shot down the pilot of your scouting plane."

"I remember," Higgins said grimly.

"Of course, we could surrender," Craig suggested.

"How would you like to go to hell?" Higgins said.

"It was only an idea," Craig grinned. "But I don't like this business. We don't know what we're trying to avoid fighting, or what strength they have, or how they will attack, if they attack."

"I don't like it either," Higgins answered. "But I didn't choose it. Damn them, if they're going to attack, I wish they would get on with it!"

Over the huge ship the tiny plane circled. Every man on the Idaho knew the situation was nasty. They were being watched. There was nothing they could do to stop it. The shadowing plane was above anti-aircraft fire. The warship could not hide from it. There was no protecting destroyer to lay a friendly smoke screen to shield them from the eyes in the sky. Meanwhile, somewhere around them a hidden enemy might be marshalling forces to destroy them.

"Have you tried to contact them?" Craig asked.

"I tried to reach them by radio all last night," Higgins answered. "There was no answer. The radio operators say there are no signals in the air. This, plus the fact that they have not attempted to answer our signals, forces me to the conclusion that they have not discovered radio. Of course they may use wave bands beyond the range of out receivers—Hello! What's that?"

From somewhere near them a shout had sounded.

Leaning over the edge of the bridge, Craig saw a sailor on the lower deck. The man was also leaning over pointing down toward the sea. He shouted again and turned upward toward the bridge. His face was white with terror.

"What is it?" Captain Higgins demanded.

"It's—It's that silver stuff on the surface, sir," the sailor answered. "It's—it's eating the sides of the ship sir. It's eating the ship."

The Idaho was still in the area of the bright substance that floated on the surface of the sea. Captain Higgins raced from the bridge down to the main deck. Craig followed him. By the time they reached the spot where the sailor was standing several other officers had gathered. They were all staring down at the sea.

Craig leaned over the rail, looked down. Horror tightened an iron band around his heart.

At the waterline, a great gash had been eaten into the steel hull of the Idaho. The plates of the ship were the best grade of chrome steel, heat-treated and hardened. They were designed to withstand the battering of sixteen-inch shells. The steel in them was the toughest metal that had ever come out of Pittsburgh.

Where the oily, shiny substance touched it, the steel was crumbling away.

"Acid!" Craig heard an officer gasp. "That's what the silver stuff is. Acid! They sprayed it on the sea."

"They plotted our course and set a booby-trap for us."

"That can't be an acid," someone protested. "It is impossible to secure a concentration of acid on the surface of the sea strong enough to eat holes in steel."

"Maybe it's impossible but it sure as hell has happened!"

Each passing wave tossed the oily liquid against the hull of the Idaho. It hissed softly when it struck and promptly began its deadly work. What was happening below the waterline was not visible. Probably no damage was being done there because the acid was on the surface and did not touch the areas below the waterline. But enough damage was being done above the water! Pits two inches deep were already appearing in the steel sides of the ship.

"Full speed ahead!" Captain Higgins ordered.

Their hope was to get out of the area covered by the acid and to get out of it quickly. But—the patch of silver was miles in extent. And there was no way to determine exactly how much damage had been done to the ship. The line of corrosion extending around the hull might have weakened her so badly that she was unseaworthy.

Captain Higgins took the only possible course. He ordered the ship to make for land.

Two hours later the Idaho was resting in a natural harbor between low hills. A river emptied into the sea here. Captain Higgins had grown years older as he took the ship into the mouth of the harbor. He had no charts of the place, no way of knowing how much water was available, or whether there were hidden reefs waiting to rip the bottom out of the ship. He took her in blind, the hardest job any ship's master ever has to face.

Like a wounded lion, the Idaho was seeking a place where she could lie up and determine how badly she had been hurt. In entering the harbor she was going into what might easily be a death trap but if she stayed outside, her weakened hull might give away and she might go down with all hands.

Higgins sent his engineers in boats to determine how much damage had been done to the hull. With his officers, he waited on the bridge for the engineers to report. There was none of the acid on the surface of the harbor.

Craig heard the chief engineer report.

"The hull is so weak that the ship may sink at any moment, sir. An effort to move her might crumble the plates. Holes in the sides six to eight inches deep, sir."

The captain's hands on the rail of the bridge tightened until the knuckles showed white.

"Very well," he said. "Beach her."

"Beach her, sir?"

"Yes. If we stay here, we may find more of that acid sprayed on the water, in which case the ship will sink."

The crew began preparations to carry out the orders. The Idaho was done, finished, ended.

High overhead the single watchful plane still circled.

Higgins shook his fist at it. "Damn you—" he said. "Damn you—"

The Idaho was carefully brought into the mouth of the river until she touched bottom. Fortunately the bottom was sandy mud. The ship sighed and settled herself into it like a tired sea monster coming out of the ocean to die. Everyone on board her knew that this was the ship's last resting place. Her steel bones would remain here until they rusted away. As the ship's keel grated on the bottom, Captain Higgins looked like a man who is hearing his own death sentence but his back was stiff as a ramrod and his chin was high.

# CHAPTER V
# The Ogrum

"Exploring parties ashore," Captain Higgins ordered.

"With your permission," Craig said, "I should like to be a member of one of those parties."

"Certainly," the captain said. "I'll do even better than that—I'll put you in charge of one of them."

"Thank you, sir," Craig said. In accordance with the best naval tradition, he kept his voice emotionless, but his heart leaped at the thought. He was going to lead a squad of blue-jackets ashore!

He was assembling his group when Michaelson, wildly excited, came dashing up. "I understand you are taking a squad ashore!" the scientist excitedly panted.

"That's right," Craig answered.

"I want to go along."

"You want to go along?" Craig glanced toward the nearby shore. Above the swamps bordering the river one of the lizard-birds was flapping. It was carrying in its taloned claws something that looked like a small monkey. Now and then coughing grunts came from the swamp, evidence of the beasts lurking there. "You want to go into *that*?" Craig questioned.

"Certainly," the scientist vigorously answered. "This is the opportunity of a life-time. We shall have a perfect chance to observe the flora and fauna of this time. We shall see them alive. No other scientist ever had a chance like this."

"You mean you will have a fine chance to be gobbled up," Craig said grimly, nodding toward the shore. "That's jungle country."

"You are taking these men into it," Michaelson protested.

"They volunteered," Craig answered.

"So do I volunteer," Michaelson said.

"All right," Craig said, grinning in spite of himself at the impetuous way this scientist flung himself into what at best could only be a nasty situation. "Get yourself a gun and come along—" He broke off to stare at the second person who was approaching him.

It was Margy Sharp. She went directly to the point. "How about me volunteering too?" she asked.

"Well, I'm damned," Craig said.

"Does that mean I can go?"

"It does not!" Craig said emphatically. "It means I'm astonished that you should have taken such sudden leave of your senses."

"Why can't I go?" she challenged.

"Because you're a girl," he answered. "And because you would be in the way. No sale, Margy. Not today and not any other day if I have anything to say about it. You stay here where you belong."

"You damned men have *all* the fun," the girl said bitterly, turning on her heel. Craig watched her walk directly to Captain Higgins and make the same request and he observed the astonishment of that naval officer. But in spite of his astonishment, the captain was quite able to say "No."

The last he saw of her, she was leaning over the rail watching the small boat put out for shore. He waved at her. She thumbed her nose in reply.

Looking back as they neared the shore, Craig saw she was still standing at the rail. He also heard the boom of the ship's catapult and saw a plane launched into the air. Captain Higgins was sending out a plane to scout the surrounding area. Craig knew what the captain was worried about—the place from which those cursed silent airplanes came.

High in the sky, he could see one of the silent floaters keeping its vigil over the Idaho.

"We'll cross the swamp and reach the hills," Craig directed.

Shots roared in the distance as they forced the boat through the pools of stagnant water. Apparently the shots came from the other exploring parties shooting flying lizards or other creatures. Once a flying lizard swooped over their boat but it changed its mind and went on to attack something else. And, as they forced the boat through a clump of reeds and into a clear channel, something monstrous snorted near them. Loud crashes sounded in the swamp tangle.

"It looks as big as an elephant," Craig shouted. "Get your guns ready."

He could see the movement of the reeds as the beast crashed toward them. Small trees were shaking, marking its passage, then it thrust its head out of the tangle not fifty feet from them.

"It's a dinosaur!" Michaelson shouted. The scientist was wildly excited. "It's a live dinosaur."

"It's going to be a dead one if it comes any closer," Craig said grimly.

"No, don't shoot," the scientist said. "It's one of the herbivorous dinosaurs, a vegetation eater. It won't harm us."

The sailors in the boat were nervously fingering their tommy-guns and staring at the mountain of flesh that was half-hidden by the jungle growth. It, in turn, stared at them. It was bigger than any elephant that ever walked the earth, and Craig, as he estimated the size of the beast, was wondering whether the tommy-guns would stop it if it chose to attack.

"If we have to shoot, aim at the head," he whispered.

In comparison to the rest of the body, the head was small. It would present a difficult target but a hit in the head might stop the beast whereas a hit in the huge body would pass unnoticed. The dinosaur stared at them. Seconds ticked into minutes. It moved its head in a circle, sniffing the air. Michaelson wanted to get out of the boat and swim to shore so he could examine it closely.

"You stay in this boat," Craig said vigorously. "You will probably get a chance to examine all the dinosaurs you want."

Muttering to himself, the scientist subsided.

Slowly, as though it had seen all it wanted to, the dinosaur turned and went back into the swamp. The shaking of the shrubs marked the direction it had taken. Craig breathed a sigh of relief.

"I told you it wasn't dangerous," Michaelson said bitterly. "You should have let me examine it."

"Never mind," Craig said soothingly. "After we get ourselves settled here, you can have a dinosaur for a pet. Push on, men," he said to the crew. "I want to climb one of those hills and take a look around."

Reaching the spot where the boat could pass no farther, they left two men to guard it and pushed ahead on foot. The swamp gave way to rising, rocky ground covered with a thin growth of huge trees. There was a whistle in the air. Looking quickly up, Craig saw a flying lizard swoop through an opening in the trees and dive head-long at something hidden in the rocks ahead.

A scream sounded as the dragon bird dived to the attack.

There was a human element in the scream.

"That bird is after somebody!" Craig shouted. "Come on."

If he had not known it was impossible, he would have been certain that the scream he had heard had come from the throat of a woman. But there were no women here in this mad world. Dashing forward he climbed to the top of a huge rock—and looked down at an incredible scene.

He was on the lip of a rocky ravine. Across on the other side of the ravine was a hole in the rock, a shallow cave. Crouching in the back of the shallow depression was a woman. She was shielding something with her body.

In front of the shallow cave was—a man. He was not the type of man to grace the pages of a fashion magazine, but in spite of bulging muscles and heavy, uncombed hair, there was a lithe alertness about him that was appealing.

There was something else that was more appealing.

The way he was facing the dragon.

The lizard bird, all claws and fanged mouth and hooked wings, was trying to knock the man down. He was fighting it desperately. His only weapon was a heavy club. He struck heavily with the club, leaped back out of danger. The bird lunged at him. He hit it across the head and knocked it backward. The bird was on the ground. It lunged again, screaming shrilly. The man struck at it, dodged to one side, hit it again. The bird came back to the attack.

No matter how valiant the defense, there could be only one ending. The dragon was too big, too fierce, too impervious to pain, too hard to kill, to be stopped by a man with a club. It lunged again. The man struck at it, slipped, fell. Hissing with triumph, leathery wings flapping, the lizard bird leaped at him.

**The dragon was too big, too hard, to be killed by a
man with a club ... there could be but one ending**

*Rat-tat-tat-tat*—Craig let go with his tommy-gun.

*Rat-tat-tat-tat*—The other men joined in, pouring a murderous fury of cross-fire down into the ravine. The bird was almost as big as a horse. It was a fierce fighter. It would relinquish a meal when it was dead and not before. One slug would not stop it. Dozens of slugs poured into it, smashed it to a bloody pulp. Even as it died it still tried to reach the man it had attacked.

As suddenly as it had started, the shooting stopped. Craig took the smoking gun from his shoulder. The dragon gave one last convulsive heave and lay still.

The man had scrambled to his feet. The sudden, blasting fury of the gun-fire must have shocked him out of his wits. He had been facing death, bravely; and suddenly death had struck down the creature that was attacking him. He stood without moving. In the cave behind him the woman left off her whimpering.

The man was darting glances out of the corners of his eyes, seeking the source from which his sudden deliverance had come. Slowly he turned his head. He saw the sailors on the lip of the ravine across from him.

A look of almost stupefying fear crossed his face. He had faced the dragon with no show of cowardice. Now, seeing his benefactors for the first time, he looked terrified. In the cave behind him the woman had also located the humans. Without moving a muscle, she crouched against the rock wall. Craig had seen wild animals, frightened by the sudden appearance of a beast of prey, act like this. A rabbit, aware of the swoop of a hawk, would be too terrified to move. A lamb, knowing the wolf was near, would crouch trembling waiting for the final snarling leap.

"He's scared of us," Craig whispered. "Don't make any sudden moves."

The man looked up at them.

"Ogrum!" he whispered. "Ogrum—"

Very slowly he laid the club on the ground beside him. Then he stretched himself face downward beside it in a gesture of obeisance older than human history. Subject races welcomed their conqueror in a manner such as this, slaves knelt before their master in this manner—in the days before men ceased being slaves.

"He must think we're gods," Craig whispered. It was a logical explanation of the man's actions yet it did not completely satisfy him.

"He thinks we are something else," Michaelson said. "He is acting like a person who recognizes a strong enemy. He is mistaking us for somebody else. Come on. I'm going down there."

The scientist was already scrambling down the side of the ravine. Craig followed him. He recognized the correctness of Michaelson's deductions. The man had whispered "Ogrum." Then he had knelt. There could only be one explanation: he thought they were somebody else. The thought raised a question in Craig's mind: What could inspire such terrifying fear in this man? What horror walked through these jungles that a man would fear more than he feared a dragon?

Craig looked up at his squad on the bank of the ravine. "Be on your guard," he said.

"Aye, aye, sir," the answer came floating down. It was an order the sailors would not be likely to need. They would be on the alert.

Michaelson was so eager to reach the man that he dashed ahead. When Craig reached him, he was bending over the man. The scientist was wildly excited. "He is human," Michaelson was babbling. "Look for yourself if you don't believe me. See, he has all the characteristics of true man."

The scientist was acting as if he expected Craig to argue the point. The big man didn't. "Of course he's human," he said. "What's so strange about that?"

"You do not understand," Michaelson explained. "He is the dawn man. He belongs to the first race of true humans ever to appear on earth. We have found a dawn man. That is of great scientific importance. See!" The scientist pointed to the club. "He has begun to use tools but he has not yet learned to chip flint. He is pre-stone age, definitely pre-stone age, but he is also definitely human, with the capacity to learn, as is shown by his use of the club. He has already made one of the first great inventions, a club. He has not yet made the second invention, fire, or the third great discovery, how to shape stone. I cannot begin to tell you how important this is."

The scientist was beside himself with excitement. Craig grinned. Science had its thrills as well as adventure. Michaelson was apparently experiencing one of science's great thrills—discovery.

The scientist promptly began to try to communicate with the man. But first he had to win the man's confidence. This he did by talking softly and gently. The man sat up to stare in dazed wonder at the scientist. Back in the shallow cave the woman crouched without moving. Craig saw what she was protecting, a child. This was a family they had saved from the dragon. From fearful eyes the woman watched her lord and master talk to the strangers.

"His name is Guru," Michaelson said, indicating the dawn man. "I am able to understand a little of what he says. His language is as yet undifferentiated into complex grammatical forms, hence I can follow his meaning without too much difficulty. He says he has lived here all his life and that many more of his people live near here. He says they live in families. Do you know what that means?" the scientist excitedly challenged Craig.

Craig, unable to get Michaelson to leave the dawn man, had left two men to guard the scientist and had taken the others on a wide scouting trip. He had just returned.

"No, I don't know what that means," he answered.

"It means that Guru and his people have not yet reached the tribal stage in their existence!" the scientist triumphantly pronounced. "They are still in the family stage but they have not yet learned to live together in tribes."

Michaelson sounded as if he thought this discovery was of the utmost importance. Scientifically, it probably was important. But Craig had other things on his mind.

"Ask him who he thought we were when he first saw us," he said. "Ask him why he was so badly scared of us. Ask him who the Ogrum are."

Craig was talking to the scientist but he was watching Guru. When he mentioned the Ogrum, the dawn man flinched. Fright appeared in his eyes. Michaelson spoke to him, consulting a notebook in which he had already jotted down words that he had learned, and listened carefully to his reply. The scientist turned to Craig.

"Guru says the Ogrum are very bad," he said. "He says they are much fiercer than the *death-that-flies*, by which he means the bird that was attacking him when we came up. He says the Ogrum fly too, and that they are like us, only different. He says he thought we were Ogrum when he first saw us. He says the Ogrum hunt down his people, and capture them, and take them to their city, and there feed them to the monster that eats forever."

"The monster that eats forever!" Craig whistled thoughtfully. "What the devil is that?"

Michaelson repeated Craig's question to Guru. The answer came haltingly, slowly. The scientist turned to Craig. "I am not at all certain what he means. Another definition would be the bright beast that is always hungry. But I do not know what this beast is, and Guru seems unable to tell me. He has never seen it, he says, only heard about it. He is much afraid of the Ogrum."

"I don't blame him," Craig said. "But what are they?"

Guru seemed unable to grasp the meaning of this question. He showed a strange disinclination to discuss the subject. He was so much afraid of the Ogrum that he did not even want to talk about them. And yet—this fact put a worried frown on Craig's forehead—Guru was no coward. They had seen him fearlessly face the flying dragon, the death-that-flew. What was there about the Ogrum that made Guru so terribly afraid of them?

Guru seemed nervous and uneasy. He looked all around the ravine as though he sensed the presence of hidden danger. Suddenly he looked up. A single word fell from his lips.

"*Ogrum!*" he whispered. "*Ogrum!*"

Craig looked skyward. A single wedge-shaped plane was diving on silent wings through the air. His first thought was that it was diving at them. Then he saw it was passing above them, aiming at some other target. A second plane was following the first, a third was following the second. There was a whole line of them, diving silently on some secret target.

The second he saw the planes, all question of the identity of the Ogrum passed from Craig's mind. It was the Ogrum who flew those silent ships, it was the Ogrum who had attacked the Idaho, who had sprayed the strange acid on the sea that had damaged the ship. It was the Ogrum who now were passing overhead intent on some other attack.

"Out of sight, everybody!" Craig shouted. The sailors slipped hastily to cover. Craig joined them. Guru had already leaped back into the mouth of his cave.

"What are those devils after this time?" Michaelson asked.

A second later, they had the answer.

Rolling across the swamps came the sound of a thunderous anti-aircraft barrage from the Idaho.

The Ogrum were moving in to attack the warship, to deliver the last smashing blow against the stranded battle wagon! Like vultures circling a dying animal, they wheeled over the Idaho.

"Come on!" Craig said. "I don't know what we can do to help but we will go and see."

As he hurried out of the ravine he saw Guru hastily helping his mate carry the child to a higher, safer cave. Guru was hiding. The dawn man might face a flying dragon, but the Ogrum were too much for him. Craig did not blame him for hiding. He led his group hastily toward his boat.

Before they reached the place where they had left the small boat a crash sounded behind them. Turning, they jerked up their guns. In this jungle wilderness, anything might be attacking them. When they saw what was following them, they dropped the muzzles of the weapons.

It was Guru. Waving his club, he had come to join them. He was chattering excitedly.

"He says he has put his wife and little one where they will be safe," Michaelson translated. "He wants to know if we are going to fight the Ogrum."

"Tell him yes," Craig answered.

"Then he says he wants to go along," the scientist interpreted.

For an instant Craig stared at the dawn man. Guru was scared. His fright was obvious. Even thinking about the Ogrum scared him. But if his new-found friends were going to fight the devils of the jungle, he was going with them!

"There," said Craig appreciatively, "beats a fighting heart. Come on, dawn man, you've got what it takes."

With Guru to lead them and point out passages through the swamp, they made speedy time in the boat. Meanwhile, clearly audible but out of sight, the sky was filled with the thunder of guns.

"The ack-ack will knock those planes out of the sky," one of the sailors said.

"I wish I thought so," Craig answered.

"What do you mean?" Michaelson questioned.

"The Ogrum must know we have anti-aircraft defenses," the big man said uneasily. "We shot one of their planes down when they attacked our scouting flier. They know we can and will fight. If they attack us under those circumstances, it means one of two things—either they're crazy or they think they can take us in spite of our ack-ack. For all I know, they may be crazy, but I'm betting they think they can take us. Sh—" Craig listened.

The anti-aircraft barrage was thinning out. The guns were not firing as furiously as they had at first. Uneasiness showing on their faces, the sailors listened.

"Something's going wrong," one of them muttered.

"Get moving!" Craig barked. He knew too well that something was going wrong. And, as they shoved the boat through the swamp, the guns from the ship began to sound slower and slower until at last only occasional blasts showed they were still being manned.

Then the gun-fire ceased altogether.

"Perhaps we have driven them off," Michaelson suggested.

"Perhaps we haven't!" Craig answered bitterly. "Look."

They were nearing the river. Through open spaces, the harbor was visible. They caught a glimpse of the Idaho.

The planes of the Ogrum were still circling above it.

The Ogrum had not been driven off.

They had won a victory!

# CHAPTER VI
## The City of the Ogrum

Hidden on the shore, Craig and his men watched the looting of the Idaho. The planes of the Ogrum were still wheeling overhead. Dozens had alighted on the water around the doomed ship and the Ogrum were climbing aboard. Craig saw how the ship had been taken. Gas! Trails of thin white mist still floated around the vessel. The diving planes had sprayed some kind of gas on the ship. It was obviously some kind of vapor different from any known in the far-off Twentieth Century but equally obviously it was devilishly effective. Guru verified the fact that gas had been used.

"White cloud makes sleep, Guru says," Michaelson supplied.

Before the sleep had come, the guns of the Idaho had taken a toll of the attackers, as wrecked planes on the water testified. Craig saw the pilot of one of the planes, obviously wounded, signal to the other Ogrum to help him. His flier was sinking and he was unable to swim. His comrades completely ignored his cries for help. The plane sank and the Ogrum pilot, after vainly attempting to swim, went under too. There were planes near that could have rescued him and certainly some of the Ogrum saw him, but they made no attempt to help.

"Devils!" Craig said huskily. "They're devils. They don't even take care of their own wounded comrades."

"If they treat their own men that way, what will they do to their captives?" Michaelson questioned.

Craig could only stare at him in horror.

"Ask him," he jerked a finger toward Guru, "if the gas *kills* the people who inhale it."

The scientist put the question. Guru, squatting on his haunches, answered slowly.

"He says they are only asleep, that after awhile they will wake up," Michaelson said.

"God!" Craig groaned. "I was afraid of that. Ask him what the Ogrum will do with their captives?"

Again the scientist questioned the dawn man.

"He says the Ogrum will take them to their city and feed them to the white beast that is always hungry."

Craig said nothing. He turned and looked at the Idaho. The skin was drawn tight across his face and knots were bulging at the corners of his jaws. He could see the Ogrum dancing on the decks. They looked something like humans except that their bodies were distorted, out of proportion. One was tall and very skinny. Another was short and fat. A third had one long arm and one short arm. Another had a long body and two very short legs. Just looking at them, he hated them.

"Damn you," he whispered. "Damn you—"

Something touched his arm. He turned and saw that Guru had risen to his feet. The dawn man, a look of sympathy on his face, was awkwardly trying to pat him on the shoulder.

"Guru is trying to tell you that he is sorry," Michaelson said.

"Thanks," Craig said chokingly. "We—we're not licked yet."

In his heart, he knew that he was whistling to keep up his own courage when he said they weren't licked. If the Ogrum could conquer the Idaho, what could a handful of sailors do against them? True, there were several exploring parties ashore, but all of them did not total fifty men.

What chance had fifty men against the might of the Ogrum? Fifty men armed with sub-machine guns when there had been more than a thousand men on the Idaho, armed with anti-aircraft cannons!

From the shore, Craig and his companions watched the Ogrum loot the ship. Oddly, they were not interested in any of the fittings of the mighty vessel. The loot that interested them was—men! They brought in large, cargo carrying planes, powered by the same weirdly silent motors, moored them in the water beside the ship, then one by one carried the sleep-stricken members of the crew to the side and dumped them into the cargo planes. Craig thought he saw them drop Margy Sharp into one of the planes. He sat silently cursing, fists clenched. Several times the Ogrum missing connections in loading the cargo planes, with the result that the unconscious human fell into the sea. The Ogrum made no attempt to rescue the fallen men but let them float away in the current flowing from the river. Triangular fins tore through the water toward these helpless floaters.

"What the Ogrum miss, the sharks get!" Craig said fiercely. Blood was flowing down his chin from his bitten lips. The sailors with him were white-faced and grimly silent. Michaelson, after watching the scene for a few minutes, turned abruptly and walked a few feet along the shore. They could hear him being sick.

One by one the loaded cargo planes took off, carrying their loads of helpless human freight. The fighter planes buzzed after them. The Idaho was left deserted. Either the Ogrum had not known there were men ashore or were not at present interested in them.

The sun was low in the west before Craig dared to venture back to the Idaho. The other exploring parties, who had been watching from hidden spots along the shore, joined him. Silently the little boats moved toward the bulk of the deserted battle wagon.

The gas had long since disappeared from the ship. By sun-down, Craig knew the whole story.

About two hundred men, caught in the lower parts of the ship by the attack and protected from the full effects of the gas by doors, were reviving. Most of them were too deathly sick to be of any immediate use. Mrs. Miller and her baby had been found hidden in the hospital bay, safe but sick.

Captain Higgins had not been found.

Margy Sharp had not been found.

One man had been dragged, trembling, from the lowest hold where he had taken refuge—Voronoff.

On the main deck, Craig held a conference with Michaelson and Guru. The answers to the questions he asked left him with a grim look on his face. He called the sailors together.

"I have been talking to Guru," he said. "Guru tells me that the city of the Ogrum is not far from here. He says we can reach it tonight, if we go by land, and if we use the big logs that float—by which he means our power boats—we can reach it by midnight."

He paused and looked expectantly at the sailors. A little stir ran through them. They instantly grasped what he was driving at.

"Moreover," he continued, "Guru tells me that the city is usually unguarded, that the Ogrum do not bother to post sentries."

Craig watched the men closely. There was hard, bitter resentment on their faces. They had seen their comrades carted away like so many sticks of wood to some unguessed fate. All they wanted was a chance to rescue their friends, or failing in that, to avenge them.

Craig wasted few words. "I am going to the city of the Ogrum," he said. "All of you who want to go with me, step forward."

The fierce shout that answered him told him all he wanted to know. The blue-jackets were with him. Only one man failed to step forward. It was Voronoff. Craig eyed him.

"What about you, Voronoff?" he said.

"Don't be a damned fool!" Voronoff spat out the words. "We don't have a chance."

"No?"

"No! The Ogrum have planes and gas and everything else. If we jump them, they'll mow us down."

"What would you recommend that we do?" Craig asked. His voice was soft and there was a worried expression on his face. He looked like a man who is faced with a tough problem and is weighing all the possibilities before deciding what to do.

"There is only one thing to do," Voronoff snapped. "Get to hell away from here as fast as we can. Hide in the jungle. Maybe the Ogrum don't know there are any of us left alive. If we jump them, they'll know we're alive and they'll clean us out."

"Hmmm," Craig said thoughtfully. "You've probably got something there. But what about the men the Ogrum have captured?"

Voronoff shrugged indifferently. "They're done for," he said. "We can't help what happens to them."

A low growl came from the mass of sailors as Voronoff spoke.

"I suppose we really can't help what happens to them," Craig said. "But I, for one am going to try to help it. We need every able-bodied man we have. That includes you, Voronoff. Are you going with us or aren't you?"

Craig's voice was still soft and pleasant. Voronoff completely misinterpreted it.

"Include me out!" he snapped. "I'm not going."

"No?"

"No! You can't make me volunteer if I don't want to."

"But we need you, Voronoff," Craig pleaded. "We need all the strength we can muster."

"You can go to hell!" Voronoff said sullenly.

"You won't go?"

"I won't go!"

Craig glanced over the side of the ship. Dusk had already fallen but there was still enough light for him to see the triangular fins cutting the surface. He nodded toward the water. "Either you go with us, Voronoff," he said evenly, "Or I, personally, am going to throw you overboard."

Voronoff looked like a man who did not believe his own ears. A low growl of approval came from the sailors. They remembered how they had found this man hiding in the lowest depths of the ship when they had come aboard. While their kidnapped comrades had fought, he had gone to hide.

"You—you don't mean it," Voronoff whispered.

"I never meant anything more," Craig answered. "We can't have any slackers here. Either you go with us or you go overboard and take your chances of swimming ashore."

His voice was hard and flat and there was not the slightest trace of sympathy in it. There was no mistaking his meaning. Voronoff turned pale. He looked quickly around as though seeking a place to hide.

"You've got no hole to pull in after you now," Craig said. "What is your answer."

Voronoff gulped. "I'll—I'll go with you," he said.

"Good," Craig said. He gave swift orders for the preparation of the attacking party. The sailors scurried to do his bidding. He was aware that Michaelson was plucking at his sleeve.

"Weren't you being rather hard on him?" the scientist questioned.

"Maybe," Craig answered. "The truth is, I don't like him. There is something furtive about him. He impresses me as being pretty much of a rat. Besides, we need every man we can get."

"I know we do," Michaelson said slowly. "But would you honestly have thrown him overboard if he had refused to go?"

Craig shrugged. "Don't ask me such questions. I don't know the answers. Maybe I would and maybe I wouldn't."

"I see," the scientist smiled. "You're a hard man, Craig. All I can say is that in this situation we need a hard man and I'm glad we have you to lead us."

"Thank you," Craig said.

Hours later Craig stood on the side of a mountain looking down at an incredible scene. Guru, by devious paths known only to the dawn man, had guided them here. Below them lay the city of the Ogrum.

The city was located on the edge of a huge, circular bay that had apparently at some time in the remote past been the crater of a large volcano. To the east where the walls of the volcano had crumbled down was a vast swamp, a favorite feeding ground for the dinosaurs. Hundreds of the great beasts could be heard screaming and fighting in the swamp.

The city itself held Craig's eyes.

He had seen the Ogrum in airplanes, he had seen them use gas, both of which meant an advanced civilization, with a great knowledge of technology. He had expected to find a city bright with lights, numbering hundreds of thousands of inhabitants, with large factories, broad streets, and—since they used planes—landing fields.

None of these things was visible. The city of the Ogrum was unlighted. There were no wide streets, no factories in sight. There was only one large building in the city, and the buildings which apparently served as homes for the Ogrum were little better than crude huts. There was a brilliant full moon overhead, clearly revealing the whole scene.

"It's not possible!" Craig whispered to Michaelson. "This can't be the city of the Ogrum. Guru brought us to the wrong place."

The scientist questioned Guru. Craig could hear the dawn man's replies.

"Guru says this is the right place," Michaelson spoke. "He says this is the city of the Ogrum, that there is no other city."

"But with the exception of that temple, this place is a dump!" Craig protested. "I have seen Papuan head-hunters who had built more pretentious cities than this. The Ogrum have planes. You can't build planes without a complex industrial system."

"It is certainly strange," the scientist said musingly. "But Guru insists this is the place and I am inclined to believe him. You will note also that the city below us is not laid out in streets and I see no evidence of a lighting system."

"Maybe they've got a black-out on," a sailor suggested.

Guru, consulted on this point, said no, the city of the Ogrum was always dark at night. Guru had a great deal of difficulty in understanding what was meant by light, but once he grasped the idea, he insisted the Ogrum never used lights.

"Well, it's a damned mystery," Craig said. "And I'm going down there and find out about it. Guru, come with me."

Craig had spent the hours in the boats trying to grasp the language of the dawn man. He still did not understand Guru as well as Michaelson did but he could understand enough for his purpose.

"Just the two of you going down there?" Michaelson questioned.

"Yes. Any more would only increase the chances of discovery. We've got to know the lay of the land and we've got to have some idea of what we will meet down there before we attempt a rescue. We probably will not be able to make an attack before tomorrow night anyhow."

After disposing his force and ordering them to get as much rest as possible, Craig and Guru started down to the city of the Ogrum. Michaelson had to be restrained from accompanying them.

"You stay here," Craig bluntly told the scientist. "You're not as young as I am and you need a rest."

Overhead was a broad tropic moon. There was no wind. From the great swamp came the only sound that broke the silence of the night, the scream of the dinosaurs, the roaring of the great lions of this time. Below lay the strange city of the Ogrum.

Craig felt the weirdness of the scene as he and Guru started down the side of the mountain. What kind of creatures were the Ogrum? What secret lay behind their existence? They had left no mark on history as he knew it. So far as the human race knew, the Ogrum had never existed. And yet—the sudden thought was startling—there was a word in the English language that came close to describing these creatures—ogre! Ogre and Ogrum were very similar. Were these the original ogres, those mythological monsters who devoured human beings? Had the Ogrum, known, feared, and named by the dawn men, come down through legends as ogres?

The thought sent a shivery feeling up Craig's spine. Was he going down into a city of monsters? Were Stinky Higgins and Margy Sharp and hundreds of men from the Idaho held as prisoners by ogres? What horrible secret was hidden down there in that silent city?

They reached the edge of the city. It was larger than Craig had thought. Hundreds, possibly thousands of rude huts, were hidden in the jungle growth. The place smelled bad. Apparently no effort at sanitation had ever been made. A nauseous stench arose from the ground. Craig wrinkled his nose in disgust.

"Filth!" he muttered. "This place needs nothing so much as it needs burning to the ground. Where Ogrum, Guru?" he said, turning to the dawn man.

"Ogrum sleep," Guru answered. "In little caves," he said, nodding toward the huts. "Ogrum sleep."

"Where prisoners?" Craig asked. He had to rephrase the question and repeat it several times before the dawn man understood.

"In big cave," Guru said, understanding at last.

"Where big cave?" Craig asked.

"Big rock cave," Guru answered, pointing toward the large stone temple that stood in the center of the city.

"Then that is where we are going," Craig said. "Come on."

Guru hung back. Craig sensed the dawn man's fear. "What's wrong?" he asked.

"Monster that is always hungry in big cave," Guru answered.

"Ah," Craig said. The monster that is always hungry! The bright beast that eats forever! A shiver passed through him as he remembered how Guru had described whatever was in the cave. "What is the monster?" he questioned.

But Guru either did not understand or could not explain, and Craig was left with no knowledge of the nature of the monster. However he could guess that the Ogrum regarded the thing in the temple as a god and offered sacrifices to it, an impression which Guru confirmed.

"Tomorrow when sun goes," Guru said. "Ogrum feed one man to bright beast that is always hungry. Next day when sun goes feed beast again. Keep up until no one left to feed. Then go hunt more people."

Craig recognized the performance as an incredibly ancient ritual of sacrifice to ensure the return of the sun. The Ogrum seemingly had no real knowledge of the universe. Each night when the sun went down they were not sure that it would rise again. To make certain the bright light in the sky would return again, they offered a sacrifice to it.

"What do they do when they run out of captives?" he asked.

"Catch Ogrum, feed him to beast," the dawn man answered.

When they ran out of captives, the Ogrum sacrificed their own people!

"Well, we've still got to find out what is in that temple and where our people are being held," Craig said grimly. "If Guru is afraid, Guru may stay here. I will go alone."

Guru was afraid. There was no doubt about that. Craig did not criticize the dawn man for being afraid. He regarded it as evidence of good, sound sense. But, afraid or not, Guru went with him. Slipping like a pair of ghosts through the rough paths that served as streets, they entered the silent city. Guru was as noiseless as a shadow, and Craig, every sense alert, moved as quietly as an Indian. The big American knew that from any of the huts an Ogrum might emerge at any moment.

They reached the temple unobserved.

It was a bigger building than had been apparent from the mountain above. Unlike the huts, it was constructed of stone. Roughly circular in shape, a line of columns circled the outer edge. The construction was crude. The Ogrum either had not yet invented the arch or scorned to use it. Numerous holes big enough for a man to enter standing erect, but not much bigger, served as entrances. The holes were without doors, another invention the Ogrum apparently had not yet made, and Craig was again struck by the strangely warped development of this race that knew how to build airplanes and to use poison gas but still did not know how to build arches.

Unlike the city, the temple was guarded. Yellow-robed, shaven-headed sentries paced around the building keeping inside the circles of the columns.

"Friends of the bright beast that is always hungry," Guru called them. Craig decided they were priests, temple guards. He saw they were armed with spears and swords. In addition each guard carried a pouch of small, round objects that looked like grenades.

"Are those things *grenades*?" Craig whispered. But Guru had never heard of grenades. He did not understand. Nor could Craig make him understand.

Through the small dark holes that served as entrances to the temple occasional flashes of light could be seen. The light was dull, like the fitful glow from a campfire that has almost burned out.

"What is that?" Craig asked.

But Guru either did not know or, for some superstitious reason, refused to talk.

"I'm going into that temple," Craig decided. "You stay here and wait for me."

This time Guru did not insist on going along and Craig realized that the dawn man was desperately afraid of something within the temple. Craig, waiting until one of the pacing sentries had passed, darted into the nearest opening.

He knew, as he slid into the building, that there was an excellent chance he would never come out, but he had to go in. He had to know what was in there, so he could plan how to defeat it. He had to know where the men of the Idaho were held prisoner and how well they were guarded and if it was possible to organize a way for them to escape. Finally, he had to know the nature of the bright beast that was always hungry, the god of the Ogrum.

What was the monster that was always hungry? Some black leering idol on whose altar was daily sacrificed a living victim? Or was it something else, some real monster that the Ogrum believed to be divine?

Guided by the fitful flickering of light ahead of him, Craig slipped along what was in effect an artificial tunnel. He reached the end of the tunnel, and stopped, appalled at what he saw.

The temple was built like a gigantic amphitheater, like some large bowl in which athletic contests were held. Circling downward in ordered rows were tier on tier of rough stone steps. Down below him, in a huge cup that apparently rose from the solid foundation of the mountain itself was—*a seething mass of white-hot bubbling lava*!

The city of the Ogrum was located in the crater of a supposedly extinct volcano. The volcano was not extinct. It was merely inactive. Fires still seethed in its heart, and the white-hot lava, held in balance by some subterranean arrangement of pressures, bubbled up here, like a geyser that never overflows and never subsides.

This bowl of lava, rising from the volcano beneath, was what Guru called the white beast that was always hungry. It was the god of the Ogrum. In a flash Craig saw why they worshipped it and why they fed human sacrifices to it. It was bright and hot like the sun. Therefore, by the laws of sympathetic magic, a sacrifice offered to the lava was the same as a sacrifice offered to the sun. The Ogrum, creatures of the dawn world, in spite of their planes and their poison gas, had no real knowledge of science, of the laws of cause and effect. The Ogrum thought that they could assure the return of the warming and life-giving sun by offering a living sacrifice to this bubbling lava!

If their reasoning was erroneous and false, it was nonetheless hideous and real for all that. For they would certainly offer in sacrifice, here, every man taken from the Idaho, unless they were prevented by force.

Across the arena he could see a larger opening closed by a grill of wooden poles. The flickering light from the pool of bubbling lava enabled him to see faces behind the grill—the prisoners. Involuntarily he started toward them. Then he saw the company of shaven-headed yellow clad guards standing beside the enclosure.

The Ogrum were on watch!

Studying the situation, Craig could see no way by which he could effect the release of the men. He had a handful of sailors to help him. There were thousands of the Ogrum. The Ogrum had planes and if they did not have firearms, they certainly had other weapons.

"Surprise!" Craig thought. "We've got to take them by surprise, divert them long enough to release our men. Then—" He cursed softly. Presuming a sudden surprise attack enabled them to release the prisoners? What would happen then?

"They'll hit us with planes!" Craig cursed. "They'll gas us and spray acid on us, and even if we manage to get away from here, they will follow us through the air." His eyes narrowed. "Which means that we have got to blow up their hangar, destroy their planes, first of all. Then—"

A plan was maturing in his mind. He slipped out of the temple, watched his chances and darted across the open space when no sentry was near, rejoined Guru.

The dawn man was frantic with excitement. "See monster?" he questioned.

"There is no monster," Craig said grimly. "Guru, where cave where Ogrum keep riding birds?"

To Guru, the planes were merely large birds that the Ogrum rode. Craig was asking the dawn man where the hangar was located. Guru led him around the temple, pointed to a projecting wing. "Birds kept there," he said.

The hangar was open. In line with their ignorance of doors, the Ogrum had never devised a method of closing the entrance of the building where they kept—and no doubt built—their planes. An open space leading down to the edge of the bay apparently was the runway where the planes landed. Inside the hangar Craig could glimpse the strange airships of the Ogrum. Except for the regular sentries that circled the whole immense temple, the hangar was unguarded.

"Twenty men with grenades will hit the hangar first!" Craig thought. "They'll smash the planes and then they will appear to retreat. The Ogrum will follow. Meanwhile across the city, another twenty men will suddenly appear and start firing the thatch huts. The Ogrum will be confused. Before they can organize themselves, I'll take a hundred men and hit the temple. By God, it will work!

"Then," Craig thought, "we'll die one at a time as we try to make our getaway. The Ogrum, even without planes, will hunt us through the jungle forever." He paused, seeking a solution to that difficulty. To free the prisoners only to have everybody perish from the relentless attack of the Ogrum would be no gain.

"The only way to keep the Ogrum from pursuing us is to destroy them—utterly!" Craig thought grimly. He had no qualms about destroying the Ogrum, if he could. The only problem was how! He had not enough men and not enough strength to meet them in open battle. Yet they had to be destroyed.

"Return to others," he told Guru.

The dawn man returned by a different route, passing through the other edge of the city of the Ogrum. Here they found a heavy stone wall, like the retaining dike of a river.

"Why wall, Guru?" Craig questioned.

"Keep earth-shakers out of Ogrum squatting place," the dawn man answered. "Earth-shakers" was Guru's name for the dinosaurs and "squatting place" was his word for city. Beyond the wall was the vast swamp. The Ogrum had erected the wall to keep the dinosaurs out of their city.

"Well, I'm damned," said Craig thoughtfully. "I wonder. Hurry, Guru. Must get back before sun rise."

At a swift trot, the dawn man led him up the mountain.

"This is what we're going to do," Craig said excitedly to Michaelson. The sailors, listening closely, squatted around him in the darkness. Dawn was not far off. Already the sky in the east was beginning to turn gray.

Swiftly he outlined his plan of attack, submitted it to the scientist. "I am no military strategist," Michaelson said slowly. "I am not competent to criticize your suggestions."

"I am," a voice spoke. "I've studied military strategy. Your plan hasn't got a chance in a thousand to succeed. You are just getting us all killed for nothing."

It was Voronoff who spoke.

"That may be true," Craig admitted. "If you have a better plan, I'm willing to listen."

"I've told you all along the only thing to do is to clear out of here as fast as we can."

"That is the one thing we're not going to do," Craig said icily. "If you have nothing constructive to offer, keep your damned mouth shut."

Voronoff sullenly walked away.

Craig selected a group to charge the hangar where the planes were kept, a second group to provide a diversionary attack across the city, and a third group to hit the temple and release the prisoners. The attack was to start just after darkness fell the next night. At that time, so Guru said, all the Ogrum would be gathered in the temple to watch the sacrifice.

"And after that," Michaelson said slowly. "What is to happen?"

"Ah," said Craig. "There is the heart of the affair. What happens next will determine whether any of us ever get out of here alive. And," he looked steadily at the scientist, "that is where you come in."

"I? What am I to do?"

"You and Guru are going to take a dozen men and round up as many of Guru's people as you can find. Here is what you and Guru are going to do."

In great detail Craig outlined the part the scientist and the dawn man were to play in the attack on the Ogrum. They made an odd pair. Michaelson, almost a physical weakling but possessed of one of the keenest minds of the Twentieth Century; Guru, a splendidly muscled giant but almost a child mentally.

"Do—do you think our part in the attack will really work?" the scientist hesitantly asked.

"It's got to work," Craig said bluntly. "If it doesn't work, we are all dead men."

# CHAPTER VII
# The Attack

At dusk a drum began to boom in the temple of the Ogrum. The sun was just on the edge of the horizon. It hung in the sky as if it hesitated to take the plunge below the rim of the world. Crouched hidden on the mountainside as near the city as he dared take his men, Craig could see the Ogrum, at the signal of the drum, start hurrying toward the temple as if they were eagerly anticipating the hellish sacrifice soon to take place.

To one side, beyond the notch in the mountains, was the swamp where the dinosaurs fed. Already the sound of the great beasts fighting and screaming could be heard.

All day long the Americans had remained in hiding near the city. Fortunately none of the Ogrum had ventured to climb the mountain. Craig had spent the day mercilessly rehearsing his men in the part they were to play until they were perfect in their parts, or as perfect as they could become in the short time available. The whole plan of attack depended on split-second timing. If everything worked right, if everybody did his job at the proper time, there was a chance that the attack would be successful. If anything went wrong—Craig preferred not to think about that. Around him, he could feel a tenseness creep over his men as the zero hour approached.

The Ogrum, as if driven by the quickening beat of the drum, disappeared within the temple.

The sun, making up its mind at last, plunged below the line of the sky.

Zero hour!

Craig could not see them but he knew that men had leaped from hiding and were running toward the projecting wing of the temple that formed the plane hangar. His fingers gripped the stock of the tommy-gun so tightly the knuckles showed white. They had to get that hangar, first. The planes had to be destroyed. Several times during the day he had seen planes take off. All had returned by night.

The vultures were in their nest.

Boom, boom-boom, BOOM, boom.

Craig almost sobbed at the sound. Grenades exploding! Grenades flung into the hangar by the attacking group. Grenades blasting among the mystery planes of the Ogrum!

Boom, boom, boom-boom-boom! Grenades exploding like a chain of giant firecrackers. In the hot darkness Craig caught glimpses of flashes of light as the grenades detonated.

Boom, boom, boom, boom-boom!

The flat sullen thuds echoed up the side of the mountain. From the darkness where the sailors crouched a low cheer arose. The men there in the night knew the meaning of those explosions.

Craig held his breath, waiting. The attack was on. Now, no matter what happened, it was too late to withdraw. Now it was kill or be killed, fight or be struck down, destroy or be destroyed. With the knowledge of the savage sacrifice about to take place within the temple, there was no question of the urge of the men to destroy. The Ogrum were beyond the meaning of mercy. Blast them, mow them down, kill them, destroy them utterly!

Craig waited. Tommy-guns chattered in the darkness. Grenades thundered. Then he saw what he had been waiting for. A tongue of flame licked out of the hangar.

Fire in the nest of the vultures!

The flames grew in violence.

"Withdraw!" Craig said huskily. "Get back. Draw them away with you."

He was talking to himself. The men attacking the hangar could not hear him. Their retreat was the next phase of the attack. Retreat and draw the Ogrum after them.

They began to retreat. Flames were roaring from the hangar. It was constructed of stone and the walls would not burn. Leaping tongues of fire poured out of the open door.

For a few minutes after the attack began, the drum-beat continued from the temple. The instant the first explosion had sounded, the drum-beat had faltered. Then it had caught itself and continued. But the continued explosions were unsteadying the hand of the drummer.

The drum stopped beating. The Ogrum poured from the temple. The moon had not yet risen. The burning hangar provided the only illumination. By its light, Craig could see streams of startled beast-men rushing from every entrance.

For a few minutes, they milled in confusion. Something had happened that was not on their schedule. They did not in the least understand the explosions they had heard and they could not grasp what had happened to their hangar.

Eventually they seemed to understand that they had been attacked and that the enemy was retreating. Stabbing flashes of fire from the sub-machine guns showed where the enemy was retreating.

Angry Ogrum charged the enemy.

Simultaneously, across the city, puffs of light began to appear. Spots of dancing illumination leaped from thatched hut to thatched hut, leaving behind them bright knots of light.

The knots of light grew. They spread. The spots of dancing illumination ran on ahead of them, leaving new knots of light.

On the far side of the city the sky grew bright.

Masses of Ogrum, bewildered by this new spectacle, paused in confusion. Their city was on fire. They did not understand it. They began to hurry toward the fire.

"Phases one and two of the attack are now complete," Craig said to his waiting men. "The third phase begins. Come on. It's our turn now."

The attack on the hangar, the subsequent retreat, and the firing of the city had been carried out perfectly. On the far side of the city the torch squad was still firing the thatched huts. This squad was beginning to withdraw also, pulling the Ogrum after them.

"The attack is a success!" Craig thought exultantly. "We've burned their planes and set their city on fire. Before they know what has happened, we will have rescued the prisoners. We've won!" The thought was burning in his mind. "We've won! Stinky and Margy and the lads from the Idaho will be free again!"

With him at their head, the sailors formed a wedge that drove straight at that part of the temple where the prisoners were held. To effect a rescue, they would have to enter the heart of the big building.

The old Roman phalanx, that fearsome mass of men that struck such terror to the hearts of the barbarians, must have looked something like the wedge of men that drove through the Ogrum city. The Romans were armed with spears, swords and shields whereas the sailors carried tommy-guns and grenades, but the effect was the same—a hard-driving body of men that stops at nothing.

The Ogrum were not expecting this charge. They were busy trying to put out the fires raging in their city. Meeting no organized opposition of any kind, and smashing down the Ogrum who accidentally got in their way, the sailors drove straight to the temple—and into it! Like a perfectly trained team executing a long-practiced maneuver, a strong rear guard slipped into place at the entrance. Craig, driving into the temple, was not going to leave his rear unprotected, to leave his line of retreat open to the chance of being cut.

In the vast arena there was a handful of yellow-clad guards surrounding the pool of boiling lava. All the other Ogrum had left the temple.

"Blast them!" Craig grimly ordered.

Machine guns thundered in what was probably the first temple of the sun ever built on earth! Hot lead screamed down at the guards around the lava pool. When the sailors saw the human, bound, ready to be offered as a living sacrifice to the hideous white beast that was always hungry, the priests of the temple lost what little chance they ever had of being taken alive.

The sacrifice had been prepared. The sailors had arrived at the last possible moment.

Two minutes after the sailors had entered the temple, there was not a yellow-clad priest left alive in the vast open arena in the center of the building. Craig was knocking bars from the cage where the prisoners were penned. Captain Stinky Higgins was standing behind those bars. Margy Sharp was standing beside the captain. Higgins had a strange look on his face.

"By the Lord, Craig—" was all he said when the bars went down. Craig felt his knuckles pop as the captain shook his hand.

The girl's face was paste white but she had her nerves under control. "Dr. Livingstone, I presume?" she said, looking at Craig. Then, as silently as a falling shadow, she collapsed.

"No, no, she's all right," Higgins said, in answer to Craig's frantic questions. "She has only fainted. She—all of us—have been through hell. Those damned beasts came in here and grabbed one of the men. We watched them—get ready to toss him into that pool of lava. Craig, how did you get here?"

Captain Higgins was dazed. Behind him the captives were pouring out of their prison cell.

"No time to talk," Craig said hastily. "We've got to get the hell out of here. Each of us brought an extra gun and as many grenades as we could carry. We'll have to fight our way back to the mountains—"

Already the sailors were tossing guns to their comrades who had been held prisoner. The look on the men's faces as they eagerly grabbed the weapons boded no good for any Ogrum who tried to stop them from escaping. Meanwhile Craig and Higgins revived Margy Sharp. The man who had been prepared for the Ogrum sacrifice was released.

"Everybody out!" Craig yelled.

In a long line the sailors trotted toward the passage through the temple that led to the exit. Once outside, they would reform their phalanx and fight their way through any opposition that might develop. No sound had come from the rear-guard they had left at the exit, proving that the Ogrum had not yet discovered that their prisoners had been released.

"We've won!" Craig said huskily. "We've tricked those devils and beaten them to the punch."

"You've worked a miracle," Captain Higgins said. "If we were back home, you would get a Congressional Medal for this."

"Thanks!" the big man grinned. Then the grin vanished from his face. "What's that?" he said sharply.

From the passage ahead of them came the metallic rattle of machine gun fire.

"It's the rear guard at the exit!" a sailor said. "They're shooting at something."

Craig ordered the file to halt and he and Higgins slipped forward to the exit. Through the hole that served as a doorway came a dull glow of light. The guard had taken refuge in the passage itself. An ensign came stumbling down the passage.

"It's a trap!" he shouted. "The whole place is surrounded. There are thousands of Ogrum out there. They deliberately let us enter the temple, then they closed up behind us."

"Impossible!" Craig whispered.

"So help me, it's the truth," the ensign insisted. "They deliberately trapped us. They must have known all along what we were going to try. They let us try it. We're caught, like rats in a trap."

There was no mistaking the implication of the man's words. Although he didn't say it, his tone indicated that Craig had led them into the worst possible booby-trap.

The machine guns were still firing. Dimly audible from outside came a chorus of shouting—the battle cries of the Ogrum. Craig slipped forward to the entrance, looked out. His heart climbed up into his throat.

The temple was completely surrounded. Or, as far as he could see, it was surrounded. From the number of Ogrum he could see in front, he did not doubt that the whole structure was circled. The Ogrum had stopped fighting the fires. It became apparent that they had never made any real effort to fight them but had only pretended to extinguish the blazes, meanwhile waiting for Craig to lead his group into the temple.

It *was* a trap.

But how had the Ogrum been able to set such a trap? Had they known all the time of the presence of the humans on the mountain above them? They had known something. Otherwise they would not have been able to set the trap. How had they learned of the attack? How had they known the exact way the attack would come?

"Yah!" a voice shrilled from outside. "How do you like it now, you big fat-head?"

Voronoff's voice! Voronoff was out there! Craig's first dazed thought was that Voronoff's presence outside, among the Ogrum, was impossible. He tried to remember when he had last seen the man. He hadn't seen Voronoff all day! Voronoff had not been a member of his group but he had assumed the man had attached himself to some other group!

Voronoff had not attached himself to some other group. Voronoff had come secretly to the Ogrum. It was Voronoff who, as far as he knew them, had revealed the plans of the attack to the Ogrum. Voronoff was a traitor!

"You wouldn't believe me when I said you were just getting us all killed!" Voronoff exulted. "I wasn't going to get myself killed with you fools. I told the Ogrum what you were planning. They're going to make me a chief."

In a flash Craig saw why phase one and phase two of the attack had gone off so smoothly. The Ogrum had permitted the smashing of the hangar. What were a few planes? They could build more. What were a few grass huts? They could erect a thousand others. The destruction of the planes and the burning of part of their city was a small price to pay if they could trap all the remaining men of the Idaho.

Craig cursed himself. He had not thought of the possibility of anyone turning traitor. He should have thought of it. Back there in the life-boat, while he was asleep, someone had stolen water. Voronoff was the only person who would have stooped to steal water when water meant life, and the only person clever enough to accuse Craig of the crime he, himself, had committed.

"I should have choked that dog to death!" Craig said bitterly. "I should have thrown him to the sharks."

Captain Higgins had come forward and sized up the situation. "No use crying over spilt milk," he said to Craig. "I don't blame you for not thinking of a traitor and I think no one else will blame you. The question is, what are we going to do?"

"What do you want?" Craig shouted.

"The Ogrum demand unconditional surrender!" the answer came. "They say, if you will surrender, that half of you will have to be offered to the gods, but that the lives of the rest will be spared. Who shall be sacrificed and who shall be spared will be determined by lot. If you don't surrender all of you will be taken prisoner and offered as sacrifices. You have five minutes to meet our demands."

Voronoff's voice went into silence. Craig, tommy-gun ready, strained to see the man. Voronoff was hidden. He was not likely to offer himself as a target.

"What are you going to do?" Captain Higgins asked. Tactfully, since Craig had planned and executed the rescue attempt, Higgins was making no effort to exert his own authority. "If I understand correctly, they offer half of us a chance to live, if we surrender."

"I don't believe they will keep any promise they make," Craig said slowly. "I think they are trying to trick us into surrendering. However I might be wrong. I am willing to put it to a vote. What do you say: Shall we surrender or shall we fight?"

The narrow passage was full of sailors who had overheard everything that had been said. There was a moment of silence. Then a gruff voice growled.

"I say fight!"

A chorus instantly answered the first voice.

"Fight the devils!"

"They won't ever give us a chance if we surrender."

"Fight our way out of here."

Captain Higgins listened. "They're good boys," he said, a suspicious quaver in his voice.

"All right," Craig said. "We fight. This temple is almost a fortress. In here, we can hold them off indefinitely. They don't have artillery, so they can't blast us out, and their planes have been destroyed, so they can't bomb us. We'll hold here until we have a chance to escape."

In the back of his mind was the thought that they *did* have a chance to escape. After all, phase four of the attack had not yet gone into operation. Phase four was due to start any minute now.

"To the roof!" he ordered.

By the time the five minutes of grace were up everybody was on the flat roof of the temple. The moon was just rising. It looked like a gigantic conflagration on the horizon.

"Time is up!" Voronoff yelled, from some place of concealment. "What did you decide."

"We decided you could go to hell!" Craig answered. "If you want us, you've got to come and get us."

Hiding around the temple thousands of the Ogrum could be vaguely glimpsed. Captain Higgins surveyed the scene. "We command all approaches to the building," he said. "If they try to charge us, it will be slaughter. We've still got a chance, Craig."

"You're damned right we have!" the big man answered.

"Except," the captain continued thoughtfully, "for ammunition, food, and water, we're all right."

"If we're not out of here by the time our ammunition runs out, we'll never escape," Craig answered. "However, we'll be out of here in an hour."

"I hope you know what you're talking about," was Higgins' only comment.

The Ogrum were making no attempt to attack. Craig circled the roof of the temple, seeing that sub-machine guns covered all approaches. A wind, moving from the direction of the swamp, brought with it the sound of the dinosaurs. The scene was like a setting from some fantastic movie—a full moon burning like a huge fire on the horizon, incredible beasts screaming in the night, a group of embattled humans on the roof of a temple as old as time.

"We've got them!" Craig thought. "They can't get to us and they don't dare attack. If they wait an hour—"

In some hidden spot outside the temple something went *plunk*. The sound was not sharp enough to be called an explosion. It was a plunk, like a rock falling in a rain barrel.

A small round object arched slowly through the air and hit on the roof of the temple. It also went *plunk*. No explosion. Just a *plunk*. A cloud of white smoke puffed out.

"What the devil is that?" Craig thought uncertainly. "Are they throwing grenades at us? Was the first grenade a dud?"

He started toward the grenade. A whiff of the smoke stung his nostrils, sent a warning bell clattering wildly in his brain.

"Gas!" he yelled. "They're throwing gas grenades at us. Stay away from that smoke."

The Ogrum had attacked the Idaho with their sleeping gas! The guards in the temple had carried sacks of what Craig had thought were ordinary grenades. They had been gas grenades!

*Plunk* went the projector outside the temple. *Plunk* went the grenade that struck on the roof.

*Plunk, plunk, plunk*—A shower of grenades came over. Gas swirled over the roof of the temple.

"Knock out those projectors!" Craig shouted. He leaped to the wall of the temple, began firing. All around him other guns were letting go. Up to now it had been necessary to conserve ammunition as much as possible. If the projectors were not knocked out, no amount of ammunition would do the humans any good.

The rattle of sub-machine guns was a continuous tumult of sound. Fires still burned in the city and the air was becoming heavy with smoke. All around the temple the Ogrum were lurking. They were not venturing into the open. Now and then they could be glimpsed darting from shelter to shelter.

*Plunk—plunk—plunk—*

More gas grenades hit on the roof.

Somewhere near him Craig heard a man choke and gasp for breath. Everywhere, even above the rattle of the machine guns, he could hear men coughing. Something stung his lungs and he coughed himself. The machine gun fire began to thin out as choking men dropped their guns. Craig found himself firing blindly, searching for the hidden projectors. The plunk of the gas grenades was loud in his ears.

"Tough luck," a thin voice said near him.

He looked around and saw Margy Sharp. The girl was holding a handkerchief over her nose and was trying to keep from breathing. She was swaying.

"I feel like I want to go to sleep," she whispered.

The gas was getting to her. It was getting to others, too. Many of the sailors had fallen. Some of them were trying to drag themselves back to the edge of the roof, trying to lift guns with hands that no longer had the strength for the task.

"We fought a good fight," Margy Sharp whispered. "Too bad we lost."

"We haven't lost yet," Craig gritted.

He was lying and he knew it. His only hope was phase four of the attack plan. Unless phase four went into operation within the space of minutes, they were doomed. "What the hell has happened to Michaelson?" he thought.

*Plunk, plunk, plunk,* went the grenades.

Had the scientist failed? Had something happened to Michaelson?

The night was hideous with the yells of the Ogrum. Sensing victory, they were screaming with delight. Meanwhile, all over the roof of the temple, more of the gas grenades were exploding. The wind, which had quickened to a stiff breeze, swept much of the gas away. But not all of it. One whiff of it and a man lost half his efficiency. Three whiffs and he was asleep.

A man in an officer's uniform crawled to Craig's feet, looked up at him. It was Captain Higgins.

"I—I guess this is it," the captain said.

"I guess so," Craig said miserably. The gas stung his lungs again and he coughed. Slowly, a little at a time, he could feel a deadly lassitude stealing over him. A weight was tugging at his knees, trying to force his legs to buckle. More than anything else in the world, he wanted to lie down and go to sleep. He fought against the impulse. From this threatened sleep a man would awaken all right—in the prison pen of the Ogrum, there to wait his turn to become a sacrifice to the sun.

Two or three machine guns—no more—were still firing, holding off the Ogrum horde. When those guns stopped—

The flames of the burning city danced in the night. The air was heavy with smoke. The screams of the dinosaurs were louder, as if the great beasts were excited by the conflagration in the city of the Ogrum. Craig was vaguely aware that only two guns were firing. In spite of all his efforts to resist the impulse, he sank to his knees. The grenades continued to plunk on the roof. Only one gun was firing. Beside him, Craig saw that Margy Sharp had gone quietly to sleep. She looked like a little girl who is all tired out with play and has decided to lie down and take a nap.

*Boom-boom! Boom-boom-boom!*

Five thudding explosions came through the night. They did not come from the temple, or near it. They were at least half a mile away.

The sound lifted Craig to his feet.

"Michaelson!" he screamed. He tried to look in the direction from which the sound of the explosions had come. The smoke was too heavy. He could not see.

"Michaelson—" his voice was a whisper. "For God's sake, hurry!"

There was no answer. Craig waited. No more explosions came. He sank to his knees, fighting against the impulse to sleep. He was dimly aware that the screams of the Ogrum had died into abrupt silence. No more grenades were plunking on the roof. He wondered if the Ogrum were preparing to charge the temple, to strike down all who had strength left to oppose them. He lifted himself up, looked over the edge.

The Ogrum were no longer watching the temple. They were staring in the direction of the explosions. They had come out into the open. He could see little groups of them nervously looking in the other direction.

Dimly, in the distance, he heard the beginning thunder of sound. It was something like the vague roar of a starting avalanche, a rumble, a mutter, a dim murmur growing louder. The smoke was too thick for him to see what was happening.

The murmur grew in volume. It became as loud as the roar of a tornado. The Ogrum stared toward it, trying to understand what it was. They were getting nervous, now. A few of them had started to run.

Something came through the smoke. It came in a lumbering gallop, a huge and terribly frightened beast. It saw the fires in front of it. Screaming it tried to turn back. The pressure of the horde behind carried it along.

A confused mass of dark bodies poured into the city. There were hundreds of them, thousands of them. Scared to the point of madness their one thought was how to escape. The smallest of them weighed more than two tons.

Craig, fighting against the effect of the gas, sobbed in sudden relief.

"Michaelson," he whispered. "You got there in time. You did it! You did it—"

Phase four of the attack plan had come into operation. Phase four called for Guru and the scientist to go around the edges of the vast swamp and set it on fire. Part of the swamp foliage would not burn under any circumstances. But great areas of dry reeds would burn like tinder.

The dinosaurs would run from the fires. The blazes would be set so the great monsters would have to flee toward the city. At the proper moment, the wall the Ogrum had built to keep them from the city would be blown up.

The dinosaurs would stampede across the city.

Craig remembered reading of the stampede of the long-horn cattle in the early days of the American west. Thousands of cattle, running madly, shook the earth with the thunder of their hooves, destroyed everything that stood in their way.

Not cattle, but dinosaurs, were stampeding across the city of the Ogrum.

Too late, the Ogrum saw them coming. They tried to run. The great beasts trampled them into muck. Huts, struck by the maddened animals, flew to pieces. Many of them, blinded, not knowing where they were going, ran into the temple. The great building shuddered at each impact. Voronoff, caught somewhere in that wild stampede, must have known too late that he had deserted too soon, before he knew the complete plan of attack. Either he did not know of phase four or the Ogrum had not believed him when he told them about it.

**The great beast trampled them into the muck**

For hours, it seemed to Craig, the screams of the Ogrum echoed through the city. The screams were drowned in the earth-shaking thunder of the stampede. The herd of dinosaurs crossed the city, turned and swept along the edge of the bay. By the time the last of them had passed through, the only building left standing in the whole area was the temple. Everything else had been smashed flat. Smouldering fires were rising again in the wreckage of the huts. What the dinosaurs had started, fires would finish.

When the last of the beasts had gone, Michaelson, his squad of sailors, and Guru came hurrying through the darkness. Guru was accompanied by dozens of his people, hastily recruited for the task of firing the swamp. Craig yelled at them.

"Come up here and stand guard!" he shouted. "I'm going to take a nap."

# CHAPTER VIII
## The End of Adventure

Craig stood at the rail of the ship.

The sun was setting and the long shadows of dusk reached across the world. Michaelson stood beside Craig. As usual, the scientist was excited.

"The Ogrum presented a strange case of warped development," he said. "Do you know what they were?"

"Devils," Craig grunted. He was not much interested in what the scientist was saying.

"Chemists!" Michaelson said triumphantly. "Through some freak, nature developed a type of life that had the mentality to become excellent chemists but with little or no ability in any other line. The acid they used on the Idaho, the gas they had developed, everything points to the conclusion that they were chemists. From what was left of their hangar, their planes were made of plastics—not a piece of metal in them. Even the ruined motors looked as though they were made of plastics. The Ogrum knew nothing of the wheel, the arch, or of architecture, yet they were almost perfect chemists."

The scientist sounded very pleased with himself for having made this discovery. "If you had not destroyed their temple, we might have found out more about them," he said accusingly.

On the dawn of the next day the systematic destruction of the entire city had been carried out. Hundreds of grenades had been planted in the temple and it had been demolished.

"Survival," Craig said. "We've got to live in this world and it's not big enough to hold us and the Ogrum. Certainly I destroyed their city. Some of them probably managed to escape alive. I'm not going to leave any rat's nest where they can get together again."

"Well, you were right about it," the scientist said. "The only thing is, I would have liked to know more about them."

"I know enough about them to last me a life-time," Craig said bitterly. "Oh, hello." The last was spoken to the girl who had emerged from below and had come to the rail.

"Good evening," she answered. She said nothing more but stood at the rail and stared into the gathering dusk. Craig was silent too.

"I should have liked to know how they worked those silent plane motors," Michaelson said.

"Huh? What did you say?" Craig asked.

"You weren't listening," the scientist accused. He adjusted his glasses and looked along the rail to where Margy Sharp was standing. "Ah. I see," he said.

"You see what?" Craig challenged, grinning.

"I see that my presence not only is no longer necessary but is not wanted." The scientist smiled and walked away.

Dusk came down. Craig was never quite sure how it happened but somehow he and the girl found themselves closer together. "Margy," he said, "about the water, in the life-boat—"

"Oh, that," the girl said. "If you're worried about that, I've been talking to Mrs. Miller. She was awake most of the night the water disappeared. She says she isn't certain but she thought she saw somebody crawl forward and help himself while you were asleep."

Craig sighed. All the time he had known he hadn't taken the water. The important thing was for Margy to know it.

"Look," said Craig, gesturing toward the shore-line, "out there is a new world, new lands, new places, all waiting to be explored. It's all ours, every foot of it, to be explored—"

"Ours?" the girl questioned, and her voice was very low.

"Yes," Craig said. "What I mean is—Margy—Well, you once said we were two of a kind—and—"

"I think," the girl said calmly, "that Captain Higgins has the authority to make us *one* of a kind, if that is what you are trying to say."

"That," Craig shouted, "is exactly what I am trying to say."

The dusk deepened into darkness. They were very close together now. Saying nothing, they looked toward shore, toward that vast, strange new land where no human foot had ever trod. It was in Craig's mind that this strange adventure in time was almost over. Then, as he thought of the new worlds that his sons and grandsons would have the privilege of exploring, the thought came that adventure is never over—it is always just beginning.

9 789359 324012